PILGRIMAGE

JOURNEYS FROM A MULTI-FAITH COMMUNITY

Celia Collinson and Campbell Miller

Hodder & Stoughton
LONDON SYDNEY AUCKLAND TORONTO

First published 1990

© 1990 Celia Collinson and Campbell Miller

British Library Cataloguing in Publication Data
Collinson, Celia
  Pilgrimages in a multi-faith community.
  1. Pilgrimages
  .I. Title II. Miller, Campbell III. Series 291.3'8

ISBN 0 340 49052 7

Typeset by Multiplex Techniques Ltd, Orpington.
Printed in Great Britain for the educational publishing division of
Hodder and Stoughton Ltd, Mill Road, Dunton Green, Sevenoaks,
Kent by Thomson Litho Ltd, East Kilbride.

Preface

Pilgrimages of one kind or another are characteristic of all religions, therefore, like rites of passage and festivals, they provide a further avenue for exploration in the pursuit of insights into religion. We stated in our previous books, *Milestones* and *Celebrations,* that Religious Education is not primarily concerned with passing on to pupils a body of knowledge about religious practices and ideas; it should aim to stimulate thought, encourage questions of meaning, purpose and values, and explore the areas of life and human experience which are the concern of religion in the widest sense of the term. This book looks at some pilgrimages in each of the five world faiths which are well-represented in Britain today. We have aimed not only to present facts about these important places of pilgrimage, but also to encourage students to reflect on why people make such journeys. We also aim to make them more aware of the spiritual dimension to life which is an important feature of all pilgrimages.

Space does not allow us to deal with all places of pilgrimage which might be regarded as important; we have had to confine ourselves to a selection which we feel is representative of each faith. It is our hope that as these are studied, skills will be developed which will enable students to apply new insights to other pilgrimages which they encounter. It is our hope that this study will give them clearer insights into the 'Pilgrimage of Life' which each of them is following.

Acknowledgements

The publishers would like to thank the following for permission to reproduce material in this book:

Arthur James for the Meditation from *Hear Me Lord* by Michael Walker (1976); Mayhew McCrimmond Publishing Co. for the prayer from *Pilgrim To The Holy Land: A Practical Guide* by Hubert John Richards (1982); Yad Vashem for 'The Garden' by Franta Baff from *The Holocaust*. The Scripture quotations in this publication are from the Revised Standard Version of the Bible, copyrighted 1971 and 1952 by the Division of Christian Education of The National Council of Churches of Christ in the USA.

Every effort has been made to trace and acknowledge ownership of copyright. The publishers will be glad to make suitable arrangements with any copyright holders whom it has not been possible to contact.

The publishers would like to thank the following for their permission to reproduce copyright photographs in this book:

Muhamad Ansar, p.85(bottom); Audience Planners, p.11; Barnaby's Picture Library, pp.49(bottom) and 87; Jerry Boyle, pp.63, 65 (top and bottom right); J Allan Cash Ltd, p.15; Christian Education Movement, p.82; John Cleare/Mountain Camera, p.10; Douglas Dickens, p.14; Genut Audio Visual Productions, pp.27 and 43; Sonia Halliday Photographs, pp.54, 60(bottom) and 61; Hulton-Deutsch collection, p.29; Indian Tourist Board, p.94; IPA, p.82; A F Kersting, pp.17, 60(top); Magnum/Raghu-Rai, pp.55 and 58; Middle East Archive, p.35; Campbell Miller, pp.23, 25, 26, 27(top), 29, 30, 31, 33, 38(both), 40(bottom), 41, 42, 47, 48(both), 51, 53, 56(both), 57 and 59; Bury Peerless, pp.13, 20, 22, 85 (top), 90, 92 and 93; Zev Radovan, pp.40(top), 45, 49(top) and 58(left); Carlos Reyes, pp.65(left), 66 and 67(right); Peter Sanders, p.79(both); Topham Picture Library, pp.69, 75, 79 and 89; John Twinning, pp.72 and 73.

Contents

Introduction

In every religion there are some places which are regarded as special. Usually this is because either the particular religion had its roots at that place, or some special event or experience took place there as the faith developed over the centuries. Exploring individual pilgrimages helps us to understand some significant aspects of belief or practice within each faith: it also allows us to share the insights people have gained into their religion through the experiences they have had while on pilgrimage. This book sets out to help you investigate the more important pilgrimages followed by people from each of the five major religions practiced in Britain today – Hinduism, Judaism, Christianity, Islam and Sikhism. Every pilgrimage has a story behind it and in each chapter such a story is followed by an account by a pilgrim of the experience of that particular journey.

In following the course offered by this book, you will certainly learn facts about the various faiths and their places of pilgrimage; it is our hope, however, that you will take the opportunity afforded by the study to think more deeply about why such pilgrimages are made.

Life itself is often thought of as a pilgrimage – a journey with a purpose, passing through various experiences from birth to death. Such questions which are faced on that pilgrimage are 'who am I?', 'why am I here?' and 'where do I go when I leave here?'. Hopefully the study of other people's experience of pilgrimages will help you find some answers to questions about your own personal journey on the pilgrimage of life.

1 Hindu Pilgrimages

A pilgrimage is a journey with a special purpose which usually has something to do with religion. Many religions talk of life itself being a pilgrimage and this is especially true of the Hindu religion in which it is believed that the purpose of the journey is to find **moksha,** the release from being reborn and becoming 'one' with God.

During life the Hindu has three ways to prepare for release: studying the holy books, doing good deeds and showing devotion to God. The last is the most popular way of finding moksha.

Making a pilgrimage to a holy place, of which there are many in India, is regarded as an important way of showing devotion to God and is thought to bring great blessings to those who make such a journey in the right spirit. Each place of pilgrimage has its own story, reminding pilgrims of how they should live their lives. These places may be, for example, mountains, rivers, local shrines or famous temples. In the course of this chapter we will look at a few of these.

Holy Rivers

In India, the home of Hinduism, rivers and also many lakes or pools are regarded as holy and are often places of pilgrimage. Behind the idea of a river being sacred is the fact that water is essential for all life. As a source of life it is thought to come from God and is a part of God. Bathing is also important in Hinduism because it is believed that the worshipper must be in a state of cleanliness to appear before God to worship; so washing has become symbolic of a desire for inner purity – indeed this is a symbol common to most religions. When worshippers bathe, it is also a way of offering prayers for spiritual cleanliness.

The holiest river in India is the **Ganges.** All Hindus wish to bathe in it at least once in a lifetime; many will also hope that after death, their ashes will be scattered on its waters. The river is considered to be sacred because it is thought of as the goddess Ganga who came to earth from the gods and therefore has the power to wash away sins.

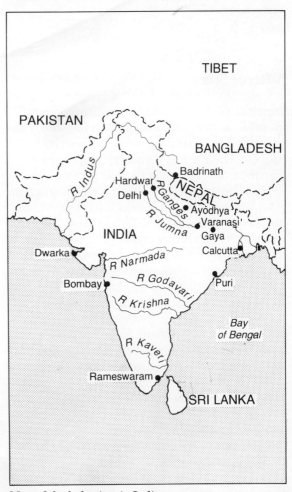

Map of the holy sites in India

7

The goddess Ganga

A River Story

Among the sacred stories of Hinduism is one which tells that the goddess Ganga was married to the gods and lived in heaven. Here she was happy and content. On earth, Sagara, the king of Ayodhya, was very discontented, because he had no sons. In despair he consulted someone well known for giving wise advice. He was told that one of his wives would give birth to a son, the other would give birth to a gourd! In time, this happened – one wife was delivered of a fine healthy boy, the other gave birth to a gourd which burst open and produced 60 thousand sons! For a long time there was great contentment in both heaven and earth. When the boys grew up, Sagara felt very powerful; to show how important he now was he decided to offer an unusual sacrifice to the gods, of a horse. The god, Indra, knew that Sagara was making a claim for great power and decided to stop him. He drove the horse away deep into the bowels of the earth.

The priests were shocked when the horse could not be found and said that Sagara's kingdom would be in great danger if the sacrifice could not be carried out. Sagara told his sons to search so they began to dig; they dug so deep that they reached the centre of the earth! At last they found the horse, grazing peacefully by the home of Kapila, one who was greatly respected for his reverence for God. The sons thought he must have stolen the horse and rushed to punish him. Kapila was angry at this interruption to his meditation and burned them all to ashes with his fiery gaze – not one escaped to tell their father what had happened.

As time passed, Sagara was convinced that some disaster had occurred. He had a grandson, the child of his first-born son, whom he sent to find out what had happened. The boy reached the home of Kapila, and bowing low he asked if he knew where his uncles might be. The boy's polite manners pleased Kapila and he told him of their fate. He also said that if Ganga could be persuaded to descend to earth and flow as a river over their ashes, they would be brought back to life.

When Sagara was told of this he meditated and fasted in the hope of making Ganga come, but his wish was not granted. When he was near to death he told his descendants that they must continue to try and persuade Ganga. It was his great-great-grandson Bhagiratha who was successful. He was so devoted to God that even Brahma was impressed and agreed to order Ganga to come to earth. Knowing that Ganga would be unhappy about this, he warned Bhagiratha that he must find some way of controlling her fall, otherwise she might flood the earth!

Bhagiratha asked for the help of Shiva and, when Ganga came rushing to earth in a angry torrent, Shiva caught the water in his mass of tangled hair. Ganga was so exhausted struggling to free herself from Shiva's locks that when he decided to release her, she came gently to earth. She divided herself into seven branches which are now the seven holy rivers of India. One branch followed Bhagiratha who led her to the sea and then to the inner regions of the earth. As

Shiva

she flowed over the ashes of the sons of Sagara, they were purified and brought back to life.

The Ganges

The river Ganges begins at the foot of the Gangotri Glacier high up in the western Himalayas. It flows 1560 miles through the plains of northern India until it reaches the Bay of Bengal and merges with the ocean. There are many holy places on its banks, and pilgrims come from all parts of India to the famous cities such as Hardwar or Varanasi to bring offerings and bathe in the waters. Later in this chapter we will look particularly at a pilgrimage to Varanasi.

There are some who make the difficult pilgrimage to the source of the Ganges and dip in the ice-cold water. Others go to Sargar Island where the Ganges joins the ocean. It is said that Sagara was told that Ganga must come to earth at this place if the souls of his sons were to be saved. Pilgrims travel to Sargar Island to make offerings of flowers which are carried out into the ocean by the tide. They pray for new life and return home

Source of the Ganges

with bottles of holy water from the Ganges.

In England, many Hindus keep a bottle of Ganges water on the shrine in their homes. Mr Bhari who lives in our community told us of the importance of the Ganges in his life.

'Every morning' he said, 'I rise early and take a bath. As I bathe I recite prayers in praise of Vishnu, Shiva and Brahma. I also ask Ganga Ma to be present in the water I use for my bath. I have been doing this every morning since I received the sacred thread, taking on the responsibilities of following my religion. Some of the words I say may tell you why I think the Ganges is important in my life.

'I say, "Mother Ganges, you grant good life and release from the cycle of birth and death according to an individual's devotion. Protect me by your compassion; O Mother Ganges, wash away all my sins." When I die, my son will make the final pilgrimage on my behalf: he will take my ashes to the Ganges and scatter them on her waters.'

Task 1
What resulted when each of the following took place?
  (a) Sagara consulted a wise man.
  (b) Sagara felt powerful.
  (c) Indra drove the horse deep into the earth.
  (d) The sons of Sagara disturbed Kapila.
  (e) Bhagiratha found Kapila.
  (f) Ganga came rushing to the earth to flood it.
  (g) Ganga flowed over the ashes of Sagara's sons.

Task 2
  (a) Why do you think water and rivers play such an important part in the Hindu religion?
  (b) Using both the story of Ganga and any other information you can research, explain why the Ganges is such a holy river.

10

Varanasi

As far as Hindus are concerned, the holiest city in all India is Varanasi, the city which is also known as Benares. It is actually known by three different names: **Kashi**, 'the City of Light'; **Varanasi**, because two tributaries of the River Ganges, the Varuna and the Asi, flow by it; and **Benares**, which is what it was called when the Muslims ruled over this northern part of India.

One Hindu legend says that Kashi was the first of all cities to be built on the earth. It has a very long history, for it was already ancient before the founding of the City of Rome; and it was certainly known as a flourishing trading centre in 500 BC.

Varanasi lies on the banks of the River Ganges at the point where the river, flowing from the north, turns and makes its way northwards again. Hindus refer to the Ganges as the great goddess Ganga. The position of Varanasi at the turning point of the sacred river gave rise to the belief that the city was especially favoured by the gods. Many pilgrims journey here and believe that bathing in the river at this place will release them from their sins. Many come to Varanasi to die, for it is believed that death in this place will bring **moksha**, freedom from ever being reborn on earth again. (Hindus believe in reincarnation, i.e. when someone dies, the soul returns to another life; this can go on through many, many rebirths until the soul comes to know God perfectly.)

The whole city of Varanasi is dedicated to Shiva, the Hindu god of destruction. Hindus say that nothing on earth remains the same: the world is constantly changing so Shiva destroys the old to create the new.

Pilgrimage to Varanasi

One of the Hindus in our community who has made a pilgrimage to Varanasi is Mrs Patel. When we spoke to her about it we asked her why she had made such a long journey to this ancient Indian city. She told us, 'I was very ill last year. During my illness I prayed constantly to Shiva to bring me renewed strength. I wanted to be able to care for my family as I always had done. I promised that if I recovered, I would make the pilgrimage which is said to bring us freedom from being reborn – that is, I would go to Varanasi and bathe in the sacred river Ganges at five holy places. I did recover and I wanted to keep my promise to be in the city of Shiva and receive his blessings.'

Our question: What about preparations for the journey? There must have been a great deal to arrange.

Answer: Yes, but my father made the arrangements for me. He wrote to relatives in India who contacted a priest attached to one of the Varanasi temples. My son and daughter accompanied me and when we arrived, it was this priest who met us at the railway station and took us to our lodgings. He also acted as our guide around the city and made sure that the religious actions I carried out were correct so that my pilgrimage would be truly successful.

Our question: We understand that there are over two thousand temples in Varanasi, most of which are dedicated to the worship of Shiva. Which of the temples you visited is most memorable to you?

Answer: That is easy to answer! The Vishvanatha Temple is the holiest in the city because it was built especially to honour Lord Shiva and was blessed by him. Let me tell you the story of this important shrine.

Pilgrims at the Vishvanatha Temple

The Story of the Vishvanatha Temple

The ancient holy books of the Hindus tell of a time when a great drought threatened to destroy the earth. Brahma, the creator god, knew that there was only one man who could bring back order to the world and save the earth from the serious drought – that man was Divodas. Divodas was a wise king who had given up his home so that he could spend time meditating on the banks of the Ganges. He wanted to find moksha – salvation – so he prayed daily at Kashi. One day while Divodas was at prayer, Brahma appeared to him, asking him to return to his throne and become ruler of the earth. Divodas agreed but made one condition: he insisted that all of the gods leave Kashi so that he could get on with his work without any interference! It was agreed: even the great god Shiva was forced to leave the city which he loved, and so Divodas became king of all the earth and order was restored.

Brahma

Shiva brooded on his exile. He really missed his city and longed to return, so he made plans to try and get rid of Divodas. First he sent his spirit servants to remove him, but they found the city so charming that they forgot their task and decided to remain! Next, he tried to show that Divodas was not fit to rule; this plan also failed. The city prospered and its people were happy.

Shiva was so despairing that the gods decided to help. They knew that Divodas was a good man and that he wanted salvation so they sent Ganesh, disguised as an astrologer, to tell Divodas that a priest would come from the north and he must listen carefully to the priest's words. The god Vishnu appeared to Divodas disguised as a priest and advised him that if he wanted salvation he should seek the special help of Shiva.

Divodas therefore built a temple in honour of Shiva. Shiva was delighted that he could at last return to the city he loved: his presence blessed the temple and so it became his earthly home.

Our question: Tell us more about this temple to Shiva; is it very large?

Answer: No, it is not very large but it is a splendid place. It has a domed roof with two spires, known as **shikharas**. One of these is plated with gold so it is often called the Golden Temple. It contains a **linga**, the symbol of Shiva, which rests underneath the shikhara and it is set in solid silver. A linga is a rounded pillar of stone or even marble. It is usually said to represent both the male creative force of the universe in which Shiva is involved and also the ancient idea that a pillar separates heaven from earth.

Our question: Presumably as part of your pilgrimage you attended worship in this temple?

Answer: Oh yes! I went both morning and evening to the temple precincts when **arati** was performed: arati is when lights are lit, waved in front of the god and then placed next to his image. We saw the linga being bathed with water from the sacred Ganges, then anointed and decked with flowers.

Interior of Vishvanatha Temple

There were hundreds of pilgrims expressing their devotion to Lord Shiva. My priest also arranged for me to make an offering as a special thanksgiving to Shiva for my recovery. Worshipping at this temple, sacred to Shiva, was certainly one of the highlights of my pilgrimage: these acts of worship, and especially making my offering, made me feel very happy indeed.

Our question: You did, however, visit other holy places, didn't you?

Answer: Certainly I did – I would not really have made a true pilgrimage if I had not. Let me tell you of them now.

Five Holy Places at Varanasi

Mrs Patel went on to tell us that she had been informed by her priest that she should visit five ghats in one day and make an offering at each of them.

Our question: Will you explain to us what a ghat is?

Answer: The word **ghat** means 'a sloping place'. These ghats originally were, quite simply, the clay banks of the Ganges, but at special places steps have been constructed to make it easier for pilgrims to have access to the holy waters. These stone steps line the west bank of the river as it sweeps in a great curve seven kilometres long.

Each ghat has its own name and is used in a particular way: each has priests present to help the worshippers carry out their devotions. Some gather on certain ghats early in the morning to offer worship to the sun, others bring offerings of flowers, rice or leaves which they scatter on the flowing waters. Some bring an offering of grain for the souls of their departed relatives. The ghats are always bustling with activity as each pilgrim goes about his or her devotions. The air is always full of the sounds of bells, prayers and chanting.

Our question: What were the names of the

13

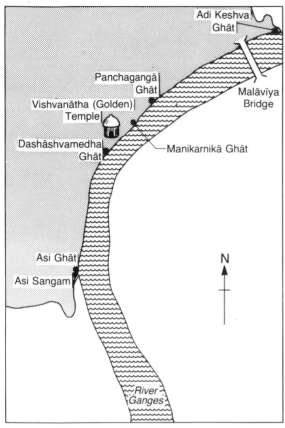

Diagram of the Ganges and the Ghats

Bathing at one of the Ghats

five ghats you visited and what was special about them?

Answer: They were called Asi, Dashashuamedha, Adi Keshva, Panchaganga and Manikarnika. These five form what is called the Panchatirtha route; each is said to help the pilgrim find a deeper meaning in life. Visiting all five is said to bring the pilgrim great blessings.

On the day I made this part of my pilgrimage I rose very early. The sky was still dark and the air a little chilly as I made my way to the Asi ghat which is holy because here the Asi river joins the Ganges. By the time I reached the second ghat the sun had risen and was casting golden rays on the water. This Dashashuamedha ghat was especially crowded for it has particular associations with Lord Shiva.

We moved on to the northern limit of the pilgrims' route at the Adi Keshva Temple where yet another river, the Varuna, meets the Ganges. After worship here, we turned down river to the Panchaganga ghat, beneath which five rivers are said to meet – the Ganges, the Sarasvati, the Yamuna, the Kirana and the Dhutapapa. At each of these holy places, in company with many other pilgrims, I bathed in the sacred waters of the Ganges, offering my worship.

The last of the five holy places, the Manikarnika, was in some ways the most interesting to visit. As I meditated at this ghat, I thought of the story of Shiva and his wife, Sati. Sati was devoted to her husband but her father despised him. He insulted Shiva by asking all the gods except Shiva to a sacrifice. Sati went to her father and pleaded with him to invite Shiva but he refused. In despair at the insult to her husband, Sati leapt onto the sacrificial fire and died. When Shiva heard of her death he claimed her charred body and carried it away on his shoulders. As he passed by where the ghat now is, one of Sati's jewelled earrings fell and landed in the well which is above the ghat. It was found by the priests who returned it to Shiva. In gratitude Shiva blessed the place and said it would be forever holy and so it came to be known as Manikarnika which means 'jewel'.

The ghat is particularly used for cremations. Piles of timber lie ready for building the funeral pyres on which the bodies are burned. At such a cremation, the body, covered with white clothes, is laid on the ghat. Mourners stand around while the pyre is lit by a close relative of the dead person. Once the cremation is over, the ashes are scattered on the river Ganges.

Durga

Cremation at a Ghat

Nearby is the great temple of the goddess Durga, one of the names for the wife of Shiva. The walls of the temple are blackened by the smoke of the fires which seem to burn constantly here. The steps are also covered with little shrines marking the places where, in days past, faithful wives threw themselves onto their husbands' funeral pyre: this custom was said to be in memory of Sati's act of self-sacrificing love for Shiva. It was altogether quite an awesome place which made one think seriously about the very important questions of life and death. Looking back on it, it certainly seemed a fitting end to my pilgrimage to Varanasi.
Our question: Did the sight of cremations at this holy place disturb you?
Answer: No, I cannot say that it did. There was really nothing morbid about the scene. There was a sadness about it, of course – there always is when someone has died. It has to be remembered that many Hindus believe that cremation at this ghat may help one to obtain salvation. I felt that just as I had made my pilgrimage to this holy place, there were other Hindus who had been brought here for their last pilgrimage, and I

15

felt happy for them that their dying wish to be cremated here had been granted.

Our question: Finally, will you sum up for us what value you see in having made this pilgrimage?

Answer: Well, I had fulfilled my promise to God and had worshipped him in this special way. I am sure it was also good for me to set aside my personal comforts for a time and all the other things which are often on my mind and which I worry about! Looking back, I feel that for this time I was able to devote myself entirely to God and I believe that in Varanasi I did find a greater sense of purpose in my life. If I never visit Varanasi again, I will always be grateful for the privilege of making pilgrimage to this wonderful, holy place.

Task 1
  - (a) Copy the drawing of Shiva and explain what his appearance says about his power.
  - (b) Collect together stories about Shiva which are associated with Varanasi.

Task 2
Explain what a ghat is and what pilgrims do at such places.

Task 3
Copy the curve of the Ganges in the diagram on page 14. Mark in the five ghats visited by Mrs Patel and write a sentence about each one.

Task 4
Mrs Patel fulfilled a promise to God when she made her pilgrimage. Can you suggest other reasons why Hindus might wish to make such a pilgrimage.

Task 5
It has been said that once you have visited Varanasi your life is never the same again. For what reasons might this statement be particularly true for a Hindu living in Britain who makes the pilgrimage?

The Four Holy Abodes

Among the many Hindu holy places are shrines situated at the northern, southern, eastern and western tips of India which are known as the four holy abodes or **dhams**. India is a vast country so these shrines are miles away from each other, and clearly visiting all four involves considerable hardship. It means sitting for hours on trains, or even walking long distances, but those who make such a pilgrimage talk of the great joy they experience when their pilgrimage is completed. Some say that it is like experiencing paradise here in the midst of this life!

The four abodes are at Badrinath, Puri, Dwarka and Rameswaram. Not all pilgrims, of course, visit all four; some may only be able to visit one of them. We will only look in detail at Puri and Dwarka which were visited by Hindus from our community.

Badrinath

The northern-most shrine is at **Badrinath**, situated high among the snowy peaks of the Himalayas, the range of mountains regarded as the home of the gods. This has been a centre of pilgrimage for thousands of years. At one time, it was very difficult to reach; even now, although transport is available, many pilgrims choose the satisfaction of walking the last 48 miles.

Pilgrims come to Badrinath between May and October as the region is snow-bound for the rest of the year.

They visit the great temple where Vishnu is worshipped in the form of **Badrinarayan**, an image with a large diamond on his forehead and a body covered in jewels.

In October the temple doors are closed. The chief priest lights a lamp filled with ghee and places it near the god. This remains lit till the day the doors are opened again and the pilgrimage season begins.

Jagannath Temple at Puri

Puri

The holy abode in the east of India is at **Puri**. This city is famous for its great Jagannath temple and its car festival, known as **Rath Yatra**. Once a year in June or July three images are brought out of the temple, placed on huge cars and dragged to the Gundicha Mandir approximately one mile away. Thousands come to Puri to take part in this event which is especially dedicated to Krishna. **Jagannath** means 'Lord of the Universe' and all Hindus, regardless of their caste, are welcome to offer their worship to him.

The Pilgrimage Story

One day the great king Indradyumma was walking by the sea shore. He saw a log floating on the water and knew that this was the one thing left behind from Krishna's stay on earth. Everything else had been submerged when the sea flooded the area in which Krishna lived. He wanted someone to carve an image out of the wood so he asked the architect of the gods, Viswarkarma to design it. Viswarkarma agreed on one condition: he was to be left completely alone until his task was complete.

The architect began his work behind the closed doors of the temple. As each day

Krishna

passed, the king grew more and more curious. Finally, on the fifteenth day he gave in to temptation and peeped in! The architect was furious, put down his tools and left immediately, leaving the image unfinished, without hands or feet. The king was most upset since he wanted to worship Krishna in the form of a beautiful image. In his sorrow, he prayed to Brahma. His prayers were answered for Brahma promised that the image would be famous even in its unfinished form. Brahma himself was present when the image was put in a place of honour in the temple; the story says that he acted as a priest and gave the image eyes and a soul.

Pilgrimage to Puri

Mr Das is a Hindu who lives in our community; he shared with us his vivid memories of a pilgrimage to Puri.

Our question: Did you make the journey especially for the festival?

Answer: It is a tradition in our family to visit the shrine at Puri. My father, who is also in England with me, often speaks of Puri and I always longed to go. Yes, I did plan my visit so that I would be in Puri for the festival – to make a pilgrimage at this time brings special blessings for the Lord is making an appearance and we wish to be present and have a sight of him.

Our question: Perhaps you will explain a little about the festival for us.

Answer: Certainly! This great temple of Jagannath has 6000 priests who perform 16 ceremonies a day to serve the three gods who are in the temple. These three are Jagannath (one of the names of Lord Vishnu when he appeared on earth as Krishna), Balabhadra his brother and Subhadra his sister. These gods are always in the temple, except for eight days in the year when they are transported to the Gundicha Mandir. Great cars or chariots the size of houses are built to carry the gods. After eight days they are returned to the temple, the chariots are broken up and pilgrims buy fragments of them to take away with them, because their contact with the gods has made them holy. It is a festival with great religious significance; the sight of Jagannath as he is pulled by the car is said to be a way of freeing oneself from sin. Many thousands of worshippers come to Puri for this great occasion.

Our question: Can you briefly describe your visit for us?

Answer: I arrived rather hot and dusty, having walked a considerable distance with fellow pilgrims. I could see the temple tower with the flag of Vishnu from quite a long way off. Already I could feel an atmosphere of excitement. I first crossed the sand dunes to bathe in the sea before seeing Lord Jagannath. As we approached the temple we saw the three huge chariots waiting for the gods. The largest was for Jagannath and was about 14 metres high and with a platform about 33 metres square. It was very colourful with even its 16 wheels brightly painted. The crowds were so great it looked as if over a million people had gathered! They were crowed on rooftops, balconies and trees. All attention was focused on the chariots, in anticipation of the moment when the priests would bring the gods from the temple.

Our question: Did you have a long wait?
Answer: Yes, I suppose I did. I arrived in the morning to be sure of a good position and it was late afternoon before the procession got under way. It did not seem a long wait, however, for we were all preparing ourselves: remember we were not waiting for a carnival – we were involved in an act of worship! I was deep in prayer for most of the time, as were my fellow pilgrims. There were also the musicians and the regular beat of their drums helped to direct our thoughts to God. Some of the women pilgrims cut their hair to offer as a symbol of giving themselves to God.

Our question: What would you say was the highlight of the pilgrimage?
Answer: Undoubtedly it was the sight of the Lord – a great roar went up from the pilgrims as the gods were placed in the chariots. Huge ropes were attached and men rushed forward to help pull the chariots; traditionally 4200 people should pull each one! As they heaved together, the chariots began to move forward slowly. I could feel the ground shaking as the great vehicles trundled along. I could understand why the word 'juggernaut' which comes from Jagannath, is used to describe heavy lorries at home! I moved forward with the crowd to throw my offering of flowers at the chariot. After it passed I fell down in the road to gather some dust from its tracks, rubbing it over my forehead as a sign that I had received the Lord's blessing. I followed the crowds until nightfall, by which time the gods were only half-way to the mandir! The journey continued the next morning after a night's rest.

Our question: Looking back on it, do you consider it was a worthwhile pilgrimage for you?
Answer: It certainly was! It is an experience I shall never forget. I saw the Lord and received his blessing in what is one of our holiest Hindu sacred places. The memory of the joy and complete devotion of the pilgrims will remain with me for ever.

The Jagannath ceremony

Task 1
  (a) What preparation did the pilgrims make for the sight of Lord Jagannath?
  (b) What were the reactions of the pilgrims when he appeared?
  (c) Who is Jagannath? Find a sentence in what you have read which you think explains why pilgrims regard a sight of him as so important.

Task 2
When Hindus speak about God they often use the word 'power'. In what ways do you think this festival would make pilgrims more aware of God's power?

Dwarka

Dwarka is the western holy abode and lies on the tip of the Kathiawar peninsula. It is the city where Krishna ruled as king and is a special holy place for that reason.

The Pilgrimage Story

According to the ancient Hindu sacred writings, Krishna came to earth to fight against evil, represented in the story by the wicked King Kansa who ruled Matharu and terrorised its inhabitants. After many years, Krishna's mission was accomplished and Kansa lay dead. There was great rejoicing in Matharu, but two men swore to take revenge for Kansa's death and continually attacked the city. Krishna and his supporters, the Yadavas, moved to Dwarka and built a fortress that could be more easily defended. The struggle continued from here and eventually Matharu was made safe, but Krishna retained Dwarka as his capital for it was such a beautiful place.

Later a war broke out between two families, the Pandavas and the Kauravas. The whole story of this struggle for power is described in the **Mahabarata**, one of the Hindu holy books. Krishna was a friend of the Pandavas and, under his guidance, they won a great victory. At the end of the battle, Gandhari, mother of the Kauravas, walked through the battle area gazing at the faces of her dead sons. In her distress she uttered a dreadful curse, saying that Krishna and all his people would die as her sons had died.

Krishna warned his people that they should leave Dwarka and they set out for Prabhasa. On the way they rested by the seashore where a quarrel broke out. Without knowing what they were fighting for the quarrel quickly became a violent struggle between two sides and eventually all lay dead, having ignored Krishna's pleas for peace. Krishna gave up the world and departed to a nearby forest to meditate on the great sadness of life; but he too was under Ghandari's curse. As he meditated, a hunter mistook him for a deer and shot him. The sea flooded Dwarka for seven days and when the flood subsided, everything associated with Krishna was gone.

Pilgrimage to Dwarka

Pilgrims who visit Dwarka say it is a joy to breathe the air Krishna breathed and to walk where he walked. To visit on a day such as Krishna's birthday is thought to bring special blessings, and Dwarka is particularly busy at such times.

Temple at Dwarka

Krishna is a god who, when on earth, was regarded as one of the people – like them, he too played music, danced and indulged in fun. Pilgrims feel close to his fun-loving spirit as they watch games which remind them of Krishna's childhood. In the evening, dancers imitate Krishna's moonlight dancing with the cow-girls, reminding pilgrims of one of the best known stories of Krishna's youth. We asked Mrs Mistry, who has visited Dwarka, what was special for her about the pilgrimage. She told us, 'The temple there is known as Dwarkanath, which is one of the titles given to Lord Krishna. It is in a very peaceful place on the banks of the River Gomati. When I visited the temple and gazed at the image of Krishna, I found myself thinking of Meera, a lady well known for her great devotion to Krishna. Meera was of a noble family in Rajasthan, but she surrendered her whole life to Krishna. Her family was annoyed with her for showing such complete devotion to the Lord so she left home and came to Dwarka to meditate in peace. Her last years were spent in this very temple. Her relatives came to take her home but she refused to go, shutting herself in this shrine while they tried to force the doors. When eventually they did gain entrance, all they found was a sari – Meera had gone. The story is that she had become one with Krishna, so great was her devotion to him. To be at the scene of such devotion filled me with awe! We show our love for Krishna by remembering the stories of his life and applying the lessons of these to our own lives; but there in that temple, I felt very close to him indeed, and aimed to surrender myself more completely to my Lord. I felt a great love for him and that experience has filled me with great hope and certainty.'

Task 3
What answer would you give, as a Hindu pilgrim, to those who may say, 'Krishna was on earth centuries ago; what good can it do today to visit places where he is supposed to have lived?'

Rameswaram

Rameswaram, a small island off the south-eastern coast of India, is where the southern-most holy abode is situated. The god Vishnu once came to earth in the form of Lord Rama: his mission was to destroy evil in the form of Ravana, the demon king of Sri Lanka. Ravana captured Sita, Rama's wife, and held her captive in his palace. Rama decided to invade Sri Lanka and save Sita. There was a great battle in which Ravana was killed and Sita was saved. On their return, the first part of India on which Rama and Sita set foot was Rameswaram.

They wanted to express their thanks to Shiva for their victory, but they needed Shiva's symbol, a **linga**, in order to worship him properly. Hanuman, the monkey god, went to the Himalayas to find a suitable

Rama

Temple at Rameswaram

stone to use as a linga. However, he was away so long that Sita moulded one and by the time Hanuman returned, Rama had already offered worship at it. In order to comfort Hanuman, Rama said that worship would always be offered first at the linga he had brought.

Rameswaram is today a very popular pilgrimage site especially for those Hindus who worship God in the form of Vishnu and Shiva. The former are known as Vaishnavites, the latter as Saivites. Worship is still offered first at the linga brought by Hanuman, and then at the one formed by Sita. Although the River Ganges is a long way from Rameswaram, all pilgrims receive holy Ganges water. The Ganges, as you will remember, is especially associated with Shiva and a regular supply of Ganges water

is brought here so that the linga can be bathed with the holy water.

Task 4
What significance do you see in the fact that besides all the other holy places of pilgrimage in India, there are the four holy abodes in the north, south, east and west?

Task 5
Consider all the Hindu places of pilgrimage which we have looked at in this chapter.
  (a) If you were a Hindu, which of these would you most like to visit as a place which would help your faith? Give reasons for your choice.
  (b) Prepare publicity for a travel agent to encourage Hindu pilgrims to visit the place you have chosen.

2   Jewish Pilgrimages

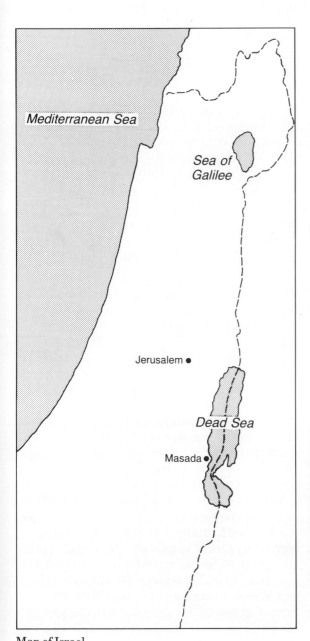

Map of Israel

The Western Wall

The Western Wall in Jerusalem is a very holy place for Jews. Many Jews living in and around Jerusalem come with great regularity to pray and chant words from the sacred Torah, Jews from all over the world also come so that they can worship at this special place. Some Jewish families bring

Distance view of the Western Wall

their sons to the wall so that they can celebrate their bar mitzvah ceremony here rather than at the local synagogue. (For information about bar mitzvah see our previous book, *Milestones*).

There is no obligation on Jews to make such a pilgrimage, but most would certainly like to be able to stand and pray at the Western Wall, for it is all that remains of the ancient Jewish Temple which played so important a part in Jewish religion, until it was destroyed about the year 70 CE.

The Pilgrimage Story

Long before Jerusalem existed as a city there was a hill known as Mount Moriah. Here it is believed, Abraham attempted to sacrifice his son, Isaac, to God, believing that he should be prepared to give God his dearest and best. (You can read the Jewish story about this in Genesis: chapter 22.) About a thousand years later, David, who was king of Israel, believed that this was an important place for sacrifices to be made to God. He wanted to build a temple on the mount but he was prevented from doing this; it was left to his son, King Solomon, to build it. According to the account in the Bible, the temple he built was a magnificent place and there was a lavish ceremony to dedicate it to the worship of God. The Jewish people believed that they had an agreement with God and there were important rules for them to obey if they would be his people: these rules we know as the **Ten Commandments**. The rules were often hard to obey fully and the people told God they were sorry, asking his forgiveness by offering sacrifices at the temple so it became the centre of Jewish worship. Here also the main annual festivals were celebrated. Indeed, some of these Jewish festivals were known as 'the Pilgrim Festivals' since Jews who were able were expected to make pilgrimage to the temple for the celebrations. In general, Jews at that time thought of the temple literally as God's house – the place where God lived among his people.

The story passes over several centuries to the sixth century BCE, when the great Babylonian Empire turned its attention to Judah and especially to Jerusalem. Many Jews were carried away as captives and forced to live in Babylon; this unhappy period in their history is known as 'the Exile'. The Babylonians destroyed the temple and many of the Jewish people felt that their faith also had been destroyed. There is one of the Psalms belonging to this period of Jewish history which shows how deeply the exiles felt.

By the waters of Babylon,
    there we sat down and wept,
    when we remembered Zion.
On the willows there we hung up our lyres.
    For there our captors required of us
    songs, and our tormentors, mirth,
    saying, 'Sing us one of the songs of Zion!'
How shall we sing the LORD'S song in a foreign land?
    If I forget you, O Jerusalem, let my right
    hand wither!

When they talked like this about Jerusalem, they were thinking of the temple which especially made Jerusalem so important to them.

Years later, the exiles were able to return home and there were half-hearted attempts at rebuilding the temple, but little was achieved until they were stirred into action by a prophet named Haggai. He told them in no uncertain manner that all the misfortunes which they were experiencing were because they were putting their own interests before those of God.

We now jump forward about another 500 years when the land of the Jews was part of the Roman Empire. The Romans allowed Herod the Great to rule for them and, in the year 20 BCE, he began to build a beautiful new temple in Jerusalem. He thought this would make him more popular with the Jewish people. You can see from the photograph of the model of Herod's Jerusalem what this temple was like.

Model of the Temple

The Jews hated to be under Roman rule and there were many attempts by some groups to rebel against them. In 66 CE an organised revolt against Rome finally broke out; it was doomed to failure and in 70 CE much of Jerusalem and the temple was destroyed by the Romans.

All that remains of that temple, built on the same holy site as those before it, is the western wall which formed part of the outer boundary of the whole temple area.

Task 1

The following are all important in the story of the Jerusalem Temple:

David	the Romans	Abraham
Herod	the Babylonians	Solomon

Place them in the correct order and write a sentence about each to say what part they played in the temple's history.

Visiting the Western Wall

Mr and Mrs Klein are Jews who recently visited Israel; we asked them to tell us about their experiences at the Western Wall. They told us that they went to the wall many times while were in Jerusalem. They said that somehow they were drawn again and again to this holy place and felt very near to God as they prayed standing close to the wall.

Our question: We understand that this used to be known as 'the Wailing Wall'; can you explain that for us?

Answer: Yes, you are quite right! Jews used to come here to bewail the loss of their temple. Indeed, there are some who say, when they see the early morning dew on the wall, that the wall itself is weeping along with mourners! For centuries, Jews have prayed that God might one day give them back Jerusalem, their holy city. On 14th

June 1967, this part of Jerusalem was recaptured from Jordan by the Israeli army and it is said that about a quarter of a million Jews walked in procession to the wall. Since that time we have no longer referred to it as 'the Wailing Wall', but simply as the 'Western Wall'.

Our question: Are there any special rituals to be followed when you visit the wall?

Answer: In many ways the wall is treated like a great, open-air synagogue so men always cover their heads at this place as they would anywhere else where they are at worship. Also, as in synagogue, men and women pray separately, so there is a partition dividing the area in front of the wall; men stand facing the wall on the left of that barrier and women are on the right. There is also a water tap on the approach to the area in front of the wall and a notice reminds us to wash our hands before going to

Washing at the wall

the wall. As I stood washing my hands when I went to the wall for the first time, feeling very excited at being at this holy place, words from Psalm 24 came to mind.

Who shall ascend the hill of the LORD?
And who shall stand in his holy place?
He who has clean hands and a pure heart,
Who does not lift up his soul to what is false,
And does not swear deceitfully.

I certainly thought of the hand washing as a symbol of my desire to come to this holy place with pure and good thoughts in my mind, so that my worship to God here might be worthy of him.

Our question: We understand that many people write prayers on pieces of paper and push them into cracks in the wall?

Answer: Yes, that is so! When we stood near the wall, we could see many of these scraps of paper, some of which looked as if they had been there for a very long time. We are told that in 1967, when this part of Jerusalem was captured from Jordan, the Israeli general, Moshe Dayan, made his way to the wall and wrote his prayer which he placed in a crack in the wall. His prayer was one word, 'shalom', which means 'peace'. Sadly, his prayer has not yet been answered for there is still strife in this land.

Our question: Since this is such an important place for Jews, it must play some part in special ceremonies. Did you witness any evidence of this when you visited it?

Answer: Many special ceremonies do take place here. In 1967 Israeli paratroopers played a significant part in the recapture of this part of Jerusalem; since then members of that part of the Israeli army are sworn in here. Part of the swearing-in ceremony is that they pledge themselves to protect 'the new temple' from its enemies; by 'the new temple' they mean the State of Israel.

A more common sight here is a bar mitzvah ceremony. We saw several taking place during our visits. We can still see the look of excitement on the faces of the boys whose special occasion it was, and the look of pride and love on the faces of their families as they watched and listened. It made our visit even more special to hear the words of the Torah echoing around that area from the boyish voices chanting the sacred Hebrew text.

Festivals also are occasions when celebrations take place here. The annual festival of **Sukkot** took place during our visit; that is the festival when we remember the journey of our forefathers as they travelled to this land after their escape from being slaves in Egypt. We saw many reminders of the festival as we passed many little shelters built in gardens, backyards or on roof tops. Such a shelter is known as a **sukkah** and is a family reminder of the temporary life of our ancestors as they made the long and difficult journey centuries ago. The eighth day of Sukkot is **Simcha Torah**, which means 'rejoicing in the Torah', and is a very joyful occasion. It marks the end of one year's readings from the Torah and the start of the next year's. At this time many groups of Jews go in procession to the wall carrying the scrolls of the Torah from their synagogues. At the wall, they dance joyfully, holding up the scrolls. We saw this on the day

A Sukkah

of Simcha Torah and the happy sound of singing and chanting still lives with us. We had, of course, taken part in such ceremonies in our synagogue at home, but it was especially meaningful to share in it at this holy place. The other memory we have of this day is seeing groups of our fellow Jews holding up **talliths** (i.e. prayer shawls) to form canopies and groups of young boys

Dancing at the wall

standing under these. They were boys who had not yet reached the age for bar mitzvah but were reciting together the words of a blessing on this special day at this holy place.

Our question: Some people might think that if you went to the other side of the wall and stood on the Temple Mount that would be more of a holy place since that is where the actual temple stood; here at the wall you are outside the ancient Temple area. Did you go on to the Temple Mount or was it always the Western Wall to which you came?

Answer: It was always the wall: you see we do not know exactly where the temple stood on the Temple Mount. In the ancient temple, the most sacred part was known as 'the Holy of Holies'. This was separated from the rest of the temple by a heavy curtain and no one ever went behind that curtain except the High Priest, and he only did so once a year on **Yom Kippur**, the Day of Atonement. Most Jews would not wish to walk on the Temple Mount for they might be walking across the spot where the Holy of Holies had been and we would feel that it was not right to do so. The Holy of Holies represented God's dwelling place on earth among his people and that is why it was such a special place.

Our question: Looking back on your visit to the Western Wall, what are your most vivid memories?

Answer: Oh! There are so many! Being there at the festival of Sukkot and seeing so many fellow Jews expressing such joy at this holy place as they danced around holding up the scrolls of the Torah certainly is a very vivid memory. In contrast to this there is also the memory of fellow Jews quietly facing the wall and murmuring their prayers, some of them, like ourselves at times, with tears in their eyes, overcome with a sense of awe at being in such a holy place.

Our question: What would you say made this visit a pilgrimage for you and not just a trip to a tourist attraction?

Answer: Undoubtedly it was a pilgrimage! This was one of our main reasons for visiting Jerusalem and we look back on it as one of the highlights of our lives. We didn't go so that when people talk about the Western Wall, we can say with pride, 'We have been there!' We went because it was a visit which strengthened our faith. It is difficult to say exactly why this is so! Perhaps it was the atmosphere of faith which one feels at such a holy place; perhaps it was the feeling of belonging to a great tradition as one stood at this ancient holy place and remembered the millions who, over the centuries, have lived by our faith; perhaps it was that as we came, full of expectations and thoughts of God, he responded and made us especially aware of his presence. Whatever it was, certainly we feel that we are better people for having made this journey, and the practice of our faith is even more important to us now than it ever was before.

Task 2
   (a) Why was the wall called 'the Wailing Wall'?
   (b) Why do Jews now refer to it as 'the Western Wall'?
   (c) Why do Jews not go onto the Temple Mount?
   (d) Why is the wall important at the time of the festival of Sukkot?
   (e) What do you think makes the wall 'a holy place'?

Task 3
Why do you think a Jewish boy would find it more exciting to celebrate his bar mitzvah at the wall rather than in his home synagogue? What disadvantages might there be for him?

Task 4
   (a) Summarise what a Jewish pilgrim is likely to do on a visit to the Western Wall.
   (b) What do you think makes such an experience a pilgrimage rather than a tourist visit?
   (c) Why do you think a Jew's faith is strengthened by visiting the Western Wall?

Masada

Distance view of Masada

The Judaean Desert stretches from the eastern side of Jerusalem all the way down to the Dead Sea. This desert is a rough, hilly, barren area, strewn with rocks. Jerusalem is some 790 metres above sea level but the Dead Sea, only 24 miles away, is 392 metres below sea-level so the journey from the city to the Dead Sea is downhill all the way. Before modern roads were made it must have been a very rough journey indeed.

Towards the southern end of the Dead Sea there stands a most impressive, flat-topped hill, some 400 metres high; its sides are steep, forbidding cliffs. At one end, it seems to taper almost to a point and from some angles appears in the shape of a ship, set down in the desert.

This lonely, rather forbidding mountain attracts thousands of visitors a year: for the Jew, it is a place of pilgrimage where he can remember a tragic yet most significant event in the history of his people. The name of this place is **Masada.**

The Pilgrimage Story

We begin the story of Masada about 43 BCE when Herod the Great saw its possibilities as a fortress and captured it from a rival who also wanted to rule the country. Herod began a massive building programme on the mountain. He dug cisterns to hold vast amounts of water, leading ducts into them from the nearby hills so that rain water would flow in. This was to make sure that there would be an adequate water supply if Masada should ever be under attack. There was so much water available from this supply that he had a spacious swimming pool and bath-house even though Masada is completely surrounded by barren desert. On the northern end of the mountain he built a summer villa in three tiers on the sheer cliff face. He surrounded the whole hill with a double wall with 37 watchtowers, making Masada a very secure fortress indeed.

Herod died in 4 BCE and the Romans, who had allowed him to rule the land even though it was part of the great Roman Empire, took over Masada as a Roman garrison.

In the rebellion of 66 CE which resulted in the destruction of the Jerusalem Temple by the Romans in 70 CE, Masada was captured from the Romans by a party of Jewish Zealots. Zealots were Jews who so much hated Roman rule that they were prepared

Herod's Palace, Masada

to fight to gain freedom. Their leader is reported to have said,

> 'For from olden times we have undertaken to serve neither the Romans nor any other lords, except God only, for he alone rules over man in truth and justice.'

Refugees from other places in the country joined them and soon there was a community of about a thousand settlers on Masada. They were not all fighting men, but included families with wives and children and they tried to live as normal a life as possible on the mountain top.

One of the most important buildings they erected was a synagogue to which they could come to offer their worship to God.

The presence of these Zealots on Masada posed no threat to the Romans so they were in no hurry to remove them and, in any case, they had other, more serious uprisings to deal with. It was not until about the autumn of 72 CE that the Roman commander, Flavius Silva, turned his attention to Masada. He approached from the side nearest the Dead Sea, setting up his command camp in a position which must have been clearly seen by the Zealots on top of the mountain. He also surrounded the mountain with eight other camps linked to each other by a wall and began, with an army of 15,000 men, the long struggle to capture Masada. Since the Zealots would not surrender, the Romans began to build a ramp on the western side of the mountain so that they could more easily break through the wall surrounding the top. They probably used hundreds of Jews captured from other parts of the land to do all the hard work of constructing the ramp. Once it was complete, they could draw an armoured tower up to the wall, from which stones could be catapulted at the defenders. Part of the tower could also be used as a battering ram to break through the wall.

On the 1 May 73 CE, the Romans managed to destroy part of the wall with fire and were sure that the next day they would capture Masada.

The Zealots were also sure that Masada would be captured. Eleazar, commander of the Zealots, gathered them all together and spoke to them.

'My loyal followers, the time has come for us to prove our determination by our deeds. At such a time we must not disgrace ourselves. In the past we have never submitted to slavery, even when it brought no danger with it: we must not choose slavery now, and with it, penalties that will mean the end of everything if we fall alive into the hands of the Romans...I think it is God who has given us this privilege, that we can die nobly and as free men...In our case it is evident that day-break will end our resistance, but we are free to choose an honourable death with our loved ones. This our enemies cannot prevent, however earnestly they may pray to take us alive; nor can we defeat them in battle....Come! while our hands are free and can hold a sword, let them do a noble service! Let us die unenslaved by our enemies, and leave this world as free men in company with our wives and children.'

It was decided. Ten men were appointed by casting lots, to kill the others, and, when the terrible deed was done, nine of them gave themselves up to the sword of the tenth. He then, after setting the palace ablaze, drove his sword through his own heart and fell dead beside the rest of his family. In all, 960 men, women and children had died; it seems that only five children and two women survived this mass suicide to tell the story to the rest of the world.

Imagine the scene, the next morning, as the Romans cautiously approached the breach in the wall expecting some resistance from the defenders, but all was deathly quiet! Then they discovered the reason as they found the bodies of the defenders, many of them huddled together in family groups. Even the Roman soldiers, hardened by the

The siege ramp

many battles in which they had fought, found it difficult not to be moved by this tragic sight. The victory they had won had now turned sour and rather meaningless. The Zealots had triumphed after all!

Task 1
Imagine you are one of the Zealots, who survived Masada, and tell your story.

Task 2
'The Zealots had triumphed after all!' Discuss this statement: do you agree or disagree with it?

Task 3
Using the description of Masada and the photographs, say what you think of it as a fortress. You should bear in mind that it is a long way from a city and is in a desert where little grows.

Task 4
You are one of the Zealots listening to Eleazar's speech; how do you think you would react to it?

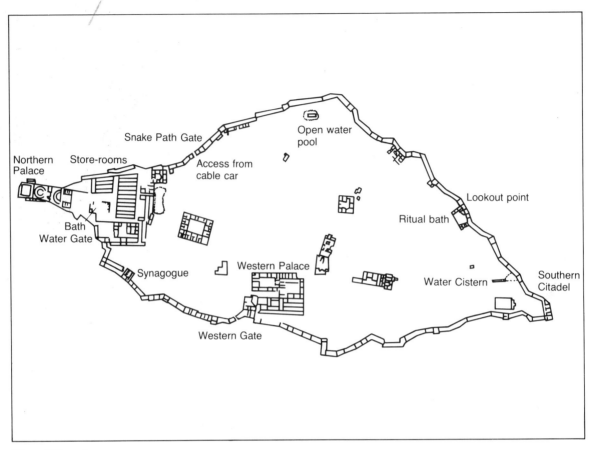

Plan of Masada

Visiting Masada

Mr and Mrs Klein regarded a visit to Masada as part of their pilgrimage to Israel. They made their way by coach down the steep road leading from Jerusalem to the shores of the Dead Sea. On arrival at Masada, they had the choice of either going to the top by cable car, or walking up the steep 'snake path', a path which is even mentioned in the ancient records telling of the Zealots' occupation of Masada. Mr and Mrs Klein chose the cable car and in a very few minutes were at the top, only to find that there was still a steep stairway to be climbed until they were on the flat summit of the mountain.

We asked them about their pilgrimage to Masada.

Our question: First of all, did you feel you were tourists visiting a place of interest, or did you feel this was really a pilgrimage?

Answer: There were, of course, many tourists, for Masada attracts thousands of visitors every year, but we certainly felt that our visit was much more than just a tourist visit – for us, it is a place we shall never forget.

Our question: But surely this is not a holy place in the same way as the Western Wall is holy, so why do you feel it is so special as far as your religion is concerned?

Answer: Among other things, it is special because here Jews were prepared to sacrifice their own lives, in so remarkable a way. They believed that to submit to the Romans was to betray their faith in God. Remember the words of their leader: 'We have undertaken to serve neither the Romans nor any other lords, except God only'. So this is a holy place, but in a different sense from the Western Wall; here we are honouring men's great faith and devotion to God, and in doing so, are rededicating ourselves to God.

Our question: Tell us about your exploration of the summit at Masada.

Answer: It really is an amazing place! We were able to form a picture in our minds of these Zealots holding out here against the Romans. We saw the storehouses which have been reconstructed, where enough provisions to last several years had been kept. We saw the great cisterns which ensured a sufficient water supply, and even baths in which these Jews went through a ritual of purification; this reminded us that these Zealots were not just fanatical nationalists, but were really devout worshippers of God. It was a sweltering hot day when we were at Masada, and we had been warned to keep our heads covered and to keep drinking plenty of water while on the summit. As we looked at the water cisterns and were only too aware ourselves of the dry heat, we imagined the Zealots gratitude to Herod for making provision for such a good water supply!

On the western side, we looked over the wall at the long, sloping siege ramp built by the Romans so that they could capture the fortress. As we stood gazing down at it, we thought of the slaves, most of them fellow Jews, who must have laboured in the burning heat to complete the ramp. We wondered what their feelings were, especially as they knew that they were working to bring about the downfall of their Jewish brothers who were defending the fortress. We also imagined ourselves as the Zealot defenders looking down on the ramp. What terror and misgivings they must have felt as they looked down and, day by day, saw the top of the ramp come nearer to the wall.

We were shown one place where the archaeologists who explored Masada found fragments of scrolls. These contained Psalms 81–85 and we were reminded of some of the words from these Psalms.

View of synagogue

Sing aloud to God our strength;
    shout for joy to the God of Jacob!
There shall be no strange God among you;
You shall not bow down to a foreign god.
I am the LORD your God,
Who brought you up out of the land of Egypt.

O God, do not keep silence;
    do not hold thy peace or be still O God!
For lo, thy enemies are in tumult;
Those who hate thee have raised their heads.
They lay crafty plans against thy people;

Let me hear what God the LORD will speak,
For he will speak peace to his people, to his
    saints, to those who turn to him in their
    hearts.
Surely his salvation is at hand for those who
    fear him,
That glory may dwell in our land.

These words must have comforted the Zealots when they were being attacked. They made us think of our faith in the same God as we stood in this place made holy for us by their great courage and devotion!

Our question: What do you think was the most memorable part of your visit? Which place on the summit would you say was most important in your pilgrimage?

Answer: Undoubtedly the synagogue! As we entered it the notice reminded us that it is the oldest synagogue in the world: that alone made us feel something of the roots of our way of life and our way of worshipping God. Here, for centuries, Jews have read the Torah and offered their prayers to God, sometimes, in the most dangerous of days, as was the case with the Zealots. As we looked over the synagogue wall, which lies not far from the siege ramp, we thought of the faith which made them worship here, with their enemies working just below, to bring about their downfall. As we stood by the pillars which once held up the roof, we imagined the sound of the Torah echoing around this small place of worship. So we sat down quietly and wondered how strong our faith would have been, had we been faced with the situation which faced the Zealots.

It is not surprising that some families bring their sons up here to this place for their bar mitzvah ceremony, for it certainly has an atmosphere of faith about it.

Our comment: Well, you have certainly convinced us that this visit was a memorable one and a pilgrimage well worth making.

Answer: Yes! As our coach left Masada and started the return journey along the shore of the Dead Sea, we looked back at the impressive sight of the mountain standing stark against the skyline and saw it as a lasting symbol of freedom, courage and devotion to God.

Our question: May we ask one last question? Were these Zealots right to commit that mass suicide? Would they not have been better to surrender to the Romans, and, even if it did mean slavery, continue with their lives?

Answer: Who can say? Only God can judge! All we can say, especially after having been to Masada, is that they were men and women of God, men and women of great devotion, and their faith lives on to be an inspiration to many generations, including our own.

Task 5
(a) Read again the words from the Psalms on page 33. Why would these verses have been particularly relevant to the Zealots defending Masada?
(b) What significance might these words have for Jews today?

Task 6
Were the Zealots right to commit mass suicide? Set out some arguments for and against what they did. You should refer to Eleazar's speech on page 31.

Task 7
Mr and Mrs Klein said, 'Masada has an atmosphere of faith about it!' What do you think they meant by that? What do you think has given it such an 'atmosphere'?

Task 8
A pilgrimage to Masada could be said to be a celebration of freedom. Explain why this could be a good description of it. What does it mean to be free? Can anyone ever be truly free?

Task 9
Israel today is surrounded by Arab nations most of which are hostile to the state of Israel. It has been said that Israel today has 'a Masada complex'. What do you think that means?

Yad Vashem

On the outskirts of Jerusalem is a large parkland with a series of buildings: it is known as **Yad Vashem**. This is a third place of pilgrimage to which many Jews make their way. It is very different from the other centres of pilgrimage like the Western Wall and Masada; these are places made holy and special by what happened at them centuries ago. Yad Vashem has been built, not to commemorate something which took place there, but so that people will always remember terrible and horrific events which happened to Jews in many different places throughout Europe between the years 1933 and 1945.

The name Yad Vashem means 'lasting memorial'; it has been built to commemorate the six million Jews who died at the hands of the Nazis, and to the many other aspects of the horrifying events which have come to be known as the **Holocaust**. Holocaust comes from a Greek word *holokauston* which means a vast or total destruction, usually by fire.

Those who visit Yad Vashem find it a sad pilgrimage; many come away somewhat tearful. They also find it a most significant experience; many say that once you have been to Yad Vashem, life can never be quite the same again.

The Pilgrimage Story

The story behind Yad Vashem begins in 1933 in Germany when Adolf Hitler came to power. He was leader of the National Socialist Party which came to be known as the Nazi party. He believed that the Germans were the 'master race'; all other people were inferior and some were so inferior that they ought to be destroyed. The largest group which the Nazis believed should be destroyed was the Jews, and Hitler made hatred of the Jews an important part of his policy. There were approximately half a million Jews in Germany at that time.

From 1933 to 1938 persecution of Jews grew throughout Germany. Jews were declared to be second-class citizens and had few, if any rights. By 1936 Jews were no longer allowed to work for the press and by 1938 they were barred from the legal professions. The night of 9 November 1938 was a terrible one for Jews. It has been called *Kristallnacht*, 'the night of broken glass', for on that night the windows of countless Jewish homes, synagogues and shops were shattered by organised rioters: 191 synagogues were burned to the ground,

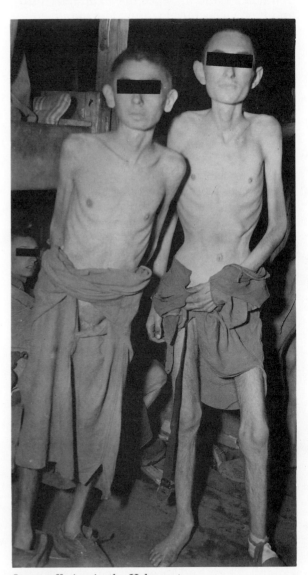

Jews suffering in the Holocaust

7,500 shops were looted and about 300,000 Jews were arrested. Terrible as these events were, much worse was still to come.

A concentration camp had been set up at Dachau. This was a prison camp to which Jews and other 'enemies of the state' were sent. Most of them never came out. Another camp was set up at Buchenwald and still more followed.

Hitler extended his power to Austria, then to Czechoslovakia, and when his troops invaded Poland in September 1939, Britain and France declared war on Germany: so began the Second World War. Hitler's armies took control of many European countries – Denmark, Norway, Holland, Belgium and France and parts of the Soviet Union – wherever they went, Jews were the target for ill-treatment. All Jews were forced to wear a yellow badge making it clear to everyone that they were Jewish. In many places where there were large numbers of Jews, they were herded together into one area of the town; where necessary, walls were built to keep them inside that area. Such places came to be known as **ghettos**. The largest of these was in the Polish capital of Warsaw. Here approximately half a million Jews were living in awful conditions, suffering from over-crowding, starvation and disease. In 1942, 300,000 Jews were taken from the Warsaw ghetto to a camp at Treblinka where they were killed. In the following year Jews living in the ghetto revolted against the Nazis but by 16 May 1943, the whole ghetto was completely destroyed. Most of those Jews who survived the revolt were later to die in one of the death camps. In 1939 there were about 3,351,000 Jews in Poland: only 369,000 of them survived the war, i.e. nearly three million Polish Jews died, of whom nearly one million were teenagers, children and babies.

As time went on, Jews from many parts of Europe controlled by the Nazis were transported to the various death camps which had been set up in Germany and Poland. These had become like factories with methods developed for gassing the victims in their masses and then cremating the bodies. Even the names of many of these camps fill people with horror as they think of the terrible deeds carried out in them – Belsen, Buchenwald, Auschwitz, Dachau, Treblinka, Sobibor, to name only a few.

In 1939 it is said there were about 18 million Jews in the world; by 1945 six million of them, approximately one third of all Jews, had been killed as the result of the Nazi's policy of hatred and death.

In 1953 the Israeli Government passed a law setting up Yad Vashem; so the 'lasting memorial' was created and has developed into the place of pilgrimage which it is now.

Task 1
Over 6 million Jews died in the Holocaust. Try to get an impression of how large this number is by the following: imagine you are standing watching as the 6 million file past you, one every 5 seconds. Work out how long it would take for them all to file past.

Task 2
Make a list of the main events in the tragic story of the Holocaust.

Visiting Yad Vashem
Mr and Mrs Klein told us that, whereas they looked forward eagerly to visiting the Western Wall and Masada, they approached Yad Vashem with very mixed feelings. They knew it would not be a happy occasion, yet they felt it was something they had to do, for they had friends who had been victims of the Holocaust. They also felt that, as Jews, their whole way of life and faith had been threatened by the horrific events carried out by the Nazis.

We asked if they could tell us why they think remembering the Holocaust is so important. We suggested to them that maybe the world is tired of hearing about such horrors; would it not be better to put it all behind us? Is there not a danger that by continuing to make so much of the Holocaust

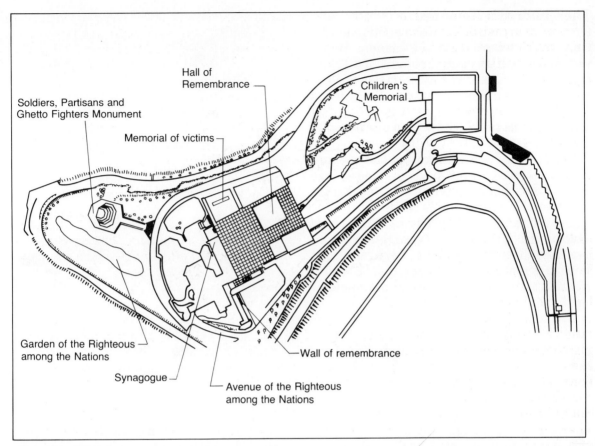

Plan of Yad Vashem

nearly half a century after it happened, Jews are just continuing to keep alive feelings of bitterness and hatred? Mr Klein replied that he was not interested in keeping alive hatred towards people; he was concerned, however, to keep alive hatred of the evil which took place. 'Think of it,' he said, 'the Jews were condemned to death as a nation, simply because they were Jews. As the Nazi armies swept through Europe, Jews were rounded up, herded into ghettos, starved, tortured and killed regardless of age. Those who did not die in the ghettos were taken to the death camps. The world must never forget this terrible deed! Six million murdered! We must keep the memory alive for our children and for their children, so that such an evil never happens again.

'We spoke to one of the Directors responsible for the Yad Vashem memorial and he said that if only it were possible, he would like to make everyone visit the memorial, so that the world never forgets. We share his view, especially after being at Yad Vashem ourselves.'

Task 3
'A place like Yad Vashem only serves to keep alive feelings of bitterness and hatred. It would be better to forgive and forget.'
Imagine a discussion between someone who takes this view and someone who opposes it.

Task 4
If you had been a victim of the Holocaust how do you think you would have wanted it all to be remembered?

The Children's Memorial

Our question: We have heard about the Children's Memorial at Yad Vashem. Will you share with us your memories of it?

Answer: The Children's Memorial is a particularly moving experience. We entered through a narrow passage in which our attention was caught by the plaque showing Uziel Spiegel who died in Auschwitz in 1944. His picture is there to represent the one and a half million children who died. The passage led into a darkened building and we held on to the rail along the wall to guide us through the memorial. On one side it was as if we were looking at a dark, but star-spangled sky, and here and there reflected in it were candles. The stars reminded us of the children who were killed; the candles were like those we light in our Jewish homes to mark the anniversary of the death of a member of the family. As we slowly moved through this memorial there was a voice, quietly reading the names and ages of the children who perished in the Holocaust.

Mr Klein said that one of the many memories which flashed into his mind as he slowly walked through, was the words of a 16-year-old Jewish boy, describing how he and his family were discovered as they hid from the Nazis; 'I think they heard the baby crying,' he said. His family pleaded with the Nazi in charge; 'Let the child go, he hasn't done anything: he is only a baby!' But the Nazi replied, 'He's only a baby now, but he will grow up to be a Jewish man. That is why we have to kill him.'

Leaving the Children's Memorial, Mr and Mrs Klein passed into the garden where they sat quietly and thought about the Holocaust children. More and more sad memories flashed before them, of stories they had read or been told. Mrs Klein told us that she remembered the story of Kitty, who was only 14 years old. Kitty had said, 'We had only been in the camp for a few minutes when Isa, a girl I had chatted to on the way to the camp, pulled me to the window. "You must see this," she said. Not fifty yards away we saw a column of people shuffling along from the railway line into a long, low hall. Once they were all inside, the door was shut and we saw an SS guard climb onto the roof, pull on a gas mask and tip some kind of white powder through an opening in the roof. We could hear screams coming from the building for a time, then all went quiet. I was witnessing murder, not of one person, but of hundreds of people at one time. We were left wondering how long it would be before we too were taken to that place of murder.'

As Mr Klein sat there in the garden, he remembered a poem written by a girl who died at Auschwitz.

> The garden
> A little garden
> Fragrant and full of roses
> The path is narrow
> And a little boy walks along it
>
> A little boy, a sweet boy,
> Like that growing blossom.
> When the blossom comes to bloom
> The little boy will be no more.

The writer was born in 1930, but was killed in 1944!

Task 5
Most visitors to Yad Vashem find the Children's Memorial an especially moving experience. Why do you think this is likely to move them more than other parts of Yad Vashem?

The Hall of Remembrance
One of the most important parts of Yad Vashem is the Hall of Remembrance. It is a rectangular building with walls built of huge boulders. It is a somewhat gloomy building with a grey mosaic floor. Inscribed on the floor are the names of 22 of the largest Nazi concentration and death camps. The Kleins told us that as they stood quietly looking at the scene, some names seemed to stand out for them – Belsen, Auschwitz, Treblinka, Sobibor, Buchenwald. Their attention was particularly drawn to the Eternal Light rising from the floor in the centre of the hall. It is shaped like a broken bronze cup and in front of it is a vault; in it have been buried ashes gathered from most of the death camps. These symbolise the burial of all the Jews who were killed, many of whose bodies were cremated in these camps.

Mr Klein told us of some of the thoughts which came to him as he stood there. 'As my eye caught the names of some of the camps, I felt anger in my heart at the deeds which had been done there. I remembered being told of a 17-year-old who described his arrival at Auschwitz. He said, 'First of all we had to strip off all our clothes. They were thrown on one side, the shoes on the other. We walked to the next room completely naked and were given our number. There, we were told by the head of the camp, "From now on you are all numbers. You have no identity. You have no place or origin. All you have is a number. Except for the number, you have nothing."'

Task 6
Describe how you think you would feel if you were treated like the 17-year-old in the above paragraph.

The Wall of Remembrance
The pilgrims moved on towards a large paved area, enclosed at one end by a high, red brick wall with magnificent sculptures set into it. This commemorates the 'Martyrs and Heroes of the Holocaust', especially those

The Hall of Remembrance

The Ghetto Uprising

who were involved in the terrible events at the Warsaw ghetto.

The wall symbolises the ghetto walls which made the Warsaw Jews prisoners in their district. The sculpture you see in the photograph is entitled 'The Ghetto Uprising', in memory of the revolt against the Nazis in April 1943. The other is entitled 'The Last March' and symbolises the final journey of Europe's Jews to the death camps.

Mr Klein told us that he and his wife stood silently in front of the wall along with many other Jews, each with their own thoughts.
Our question: Can you remember any of what was going through your minds at that time?
Answer: Oh Yes! I looked at the wall and my mind went to pictures I had seen of the ghetto wall in Warsaw; it had been rough, dirty and forbidding. Any Jew who tried to go beyond it was likely to be killed. I remembered

reading the words of a 15-year-old: 'I feel as if I am in a box. There is no air to breathe. Wherever you go you come to a gate that hems you in. I feel I have been robbed, my freedom is being robbed from me, my home and the familiar streets I love so much.' I began to understand a little of what those who revolted against the Nazis must have felt. There, before the wall, I bowed my head and honoured them for their struggle against this terrible evil.

Our question: By this time you must have been feeling thoroughly depressed!

Answer: Strangely enough we were not! For besides being faced with so many reminders of evil, we were also being reminded of the bravery and courage of those who resisted. As I looked at the magnificent sculpture of the ghetto uprising, I felt it conveyed a feeling of strength, and faith that evil cannot in the end be triumphant.

Monuments

The Kleins showed us photographs of various monuments scattered around Yad Vashem. There were two in particular which had impressed them – the Monument to the Victims of the Death Camps and one which portrays the sad figure of Job. They said that both of these, in very different ways, enriched their experiences of pilgrimage to Yad Vashem.

Our question: Tell us first about the monument dedicated to the death camp victims – it looks rather horrific to us.

Answer: Yes, in a way it does! And yet we felt drawn to it and it aroused strong feelings in us. It seemed to suggest a barbed-wire fence, and intermingled with it starved bodies, some with hands reaching out as if trying to grasp freedom. It certainly inspired thoughts of the millions of death camp victims as much as anything else at Yad Vashem had done.

Mrs Klein said that as she thought of conditions in these camps, she also remembered stories of how these people triumphed over the conditions, and how, in many cases, their religion remained of the greatest importance to them. 'Yes,' said Mr Klein, 'there is the story of Livia, a young woman who survived Auschwitz. She told how some of the girls kept track of the days, and especially the religious festivals. In December they were reminded that the

Monument to the victims of the death camps.

festival of **Chanukah** was approaching, a festival which celebrates freedom from an oppressor centuries ago. Part of the celebration involves the lighting of candles on each of the eight days of the festival.

Some of them were sent each day to work outside the camp, and as they passed a potato field they managed to hide some potatoes under their clothes. These provided a few extra calories of food for they were all very hungry. On the first night of Chanukah, however, they decided that feeding their spirits was more important than feeding their bodies: they cut some potatoes in half, scooped out a hollow in each piece, poured in a little oil which they had managed to steal, and took some threads from their already torn clothes to use as wicks. For eight days, each evening, they celebrated Chanukah, gazing at the little lamps, and humming the traditional Chanukah songs. They felt that even if death did await them, they had triumphed over those who wanted to destroy them and the Jewish faith.'

Our question: Don't you think that it must have been difficult to go on believing in God in conditions like these?

Answer: Of course it was! There are those who still find it difficult, if not impossible, to believe when they think of the Holocaust. That is why we found this other monument so significant; it portrays the sad figure of Job. As you know, there is a book in our scriptures called 'The Book of Job'. Job was a good man who met with a series of great disasters. In spite of them all, he refused to curse God. Three friends tried to convince him that his suffering was his own fault but he knew this was not true. He came very close to despair but refused to give up his faith in God. Eventually his suffering came to an end and God restored his fortunes to him.

As I stood before this sculpture of Job I remembered reading about a 17-year-old in Buchenwald who, along with some of his fellow prisoners, gathered in the cramped space between their bunks to welcome

The statue of Job

Shabbat on a Friday evening. As he whispered the words of the Shabbat Eve service, he felt as never before the real power and value of prayer and faith in God. He said it was as if his words were shattering the iron gates, going past the guards and watch-towers out into the open and reaching towards heaven.

Mrs Klein added that she was reminded of an inscription found on the walls of a cellar where Jews had been hiding from the Nazis:

I believe in the sun
Even when it is not shining

I believe in love
When feeling it not

I believe in God
Even when he is silent.

Task 7
What do you think made Mr Klein believe, as he stood looking at the sculpture, The Ghetto Uprising, that 'evil cannot in the end be triumphant'?

Task 8
Study the photograph of the Monument to the Victims of the Death Camps. Describe what you think you see in it which makes it such a moving monument.

Task 9
Find out about the festival of Chanukah. In what ways is the event it celebrates similar to the experience of Jews during the Holocaust?

Task 10
Mr Klein said, 'There are those who still find it difficult, if not impossible, to believe in God when they think of the Holocaust.' Imagine a discussion between two people, one who says he can no longer believe in God in the face of the Holocaust, and one who tries to convince him that he should go on believing.

The Avenue of the Righteous
Part of the grounds of Yad Vashem is planted with trees and is known as the 'Avenue of the Righteous Among the Nations'. Each tree is in remembrance of a non-Jew who risked his or her life to try and save Jews from death at the hands of the Nazis.

The Kleins asked how many there were and were told that at the time of their visit there were about 7,200. The Director of Yad Vashem who spoke to them said, 'Each person represented has been thoroughly investigated, for we want to honour only those who genuinely helped our people – that is the main purpose of the avenue. It does, however serve another purpose: it poses the question to the world – why were there not many, many more who saw the evil that was happening and tried to stop it?'

Mr and Mrs Klein summed up their

The Avenue of the Righteous

43

pilgrimage to Yad Vashem as follows. 'As we walked along the Avenue of the Righteous, on our way out of the memorial, we thought how important our visit had been. Our feelings were all rather mixed up – anger, sadness, and yet at the same time feeling that our faith in God had been strengthened. We were a little puzzled as to why our faith should have been strengthened! We came to the conclusion that it was because even in situations like the Holocaust, people go on believing: such evil, terrible as it was, does not in the end triumph over good. So as we left this sad, but wonderful memorial, we felt we must work harder than ever for better relationships between people, whatever race or religion they might belong to. Nothing like this must ever happen again!'

Task 11
Set out a table showing each of the main parts of Yad Vashem, and against each one describe briefly what it commemorates.

Task 12
It is said that out of every evil, some good comes. From what you have read about the Holocaust and Yad Vashem, what good, if any, do you think came out of the Holocaust?

Task 13
'Yad Vashem should not merely be a place of pilgrimage for Jews but for people of every race.' Write a few paragraphs to support this point of view. What benefits do you think people of different races could gain from such a pilgrimage?

3   Christian Pilgrimages

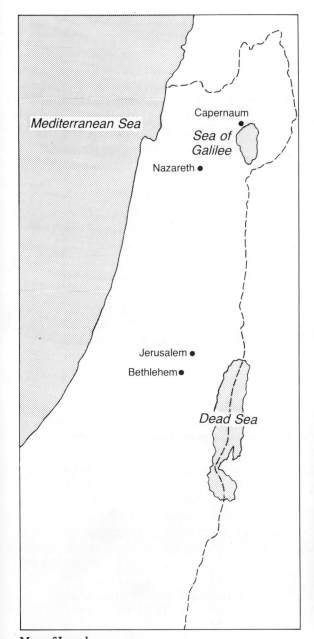

Map of Israel

Mr and Mrs Williams are Christians from our community who were able to join a pilgrimage group on a visit to the land of Israel. Israel is, of course, the land which is of great importance to Jews, but it is also a country to which Christians make pilgrimage for it is where Jesus was born and lived. It is, therefore, the birthplace of the Christian faith. We asked Mr and Mrs Williams to tell us about the most important parts of their pilgrimage. They began by telling us of their visit to the town where Jesus was born.

Bethlehem

Bethlehem is a small town which lies about five miles south of Jerusalem in the land of

View of Bethlehem

Israel. It attracts many thousands of Christian pilgrims every year and is especially popular as a place of pilgrimage at Christmas, for here in this little town Jesus was born.

The Pilgrimage Story

Mary and Joseph, the parents of Jesus lived in the town of Nazareth, about 100 miles to the north in the district of Galilee. Shortly before Mary's first child was due to be born, the Romans who occupied the land announced that there was to be a census (i.e. a registration of the whole population); and people had to travel to the chief town of their own particular tribe to register. As Joseph was a native of Bethlehem, this meant that Mary and he had to travel there. Bethlehem was extremely busy because of the census and the couple had great difficulty in finding anywhere to stay. Joseph was very worried since he knew that Mary's baby would soon be born. At last they were offered a corner in a stable and there Mary gave birth to a son. Many houses in Bethlehem were built in front of caves and it may well have been that the birthplace was a cave behind the living area of the inn, where the animals were put for shelter in bad weather.

It soon became clear that this boy was no ordinary child. In the fields outside the town, a group of shepherds were keeping watch over their flocks when suddenly, they had a vision of an angel who told them, 'Do not be afraid! I bring you good news of great joy, for to you is born today in Bethlehem, a Saviour, the Messiah, the Lord! You will find him lying in a manger.' The shepherds, after they recovered from the fear and surprise at this vision, set off for the town to visit the child. They told Mary of the vision and they bowed down before this new born baby.

Meanwhile, in another place, wise men who studied the stars had seen a new star appear in the sky and were convinced that it marked the birth of someone very special. They set out to follow the star and it led them eventually to the palace of King Herod the Great in Jerusalem. Herod was very worried at what the wise men told him, for when they talked of a new king being born, he thought his own position as king was going to be threatened. He did not, however, share his fear with the wise men but told them to go and find the child and then report back to him so that he could worship this special child as well. The wise men did find the child, and the story in the Christian New Testament says that they presented the child with gifts of gold, frankincense and myrrh. They did not go back to Herod, however, for they had a dream in which they were warned that he wanted to kill the child. Joseph also had a dream and, as a result, took Mary and the baby to Egypt, where they lived for about two years, before returning to Nazareth, where Jesus was to grow up and spend most of his life.

Herod was furious and, in a fit of mad rage, ordered the killing of every male child born in or around Bethlehem about the time of the wise men's visit. Some of the stories about the birth of Jesus may be legends which developed in later years. It may be difficult to separate the legends from the true facts, but one thing is certain – it was in this little town of Bethlehem that Jesus was born and from this birth, so too was born the faith of Christianity.

Task 1
Read the following passages from the Bible which tell parts of the story of the birth of Jesus, then answer the questions which follow each of them.

(a) Luke: chapter 1, verses 26–38. Retell in your own words how Mary discovered she was to give birth to someone special.

(b) Luke: chapter 2, verses 1–20.
  (i) How does the writer date the birth of Jesus for his readers? (verses 1 and 2).
  (ii) Imagine you were one of the shepherds. Tell your story including the vision of angels and the visit to see the child Jesus.

(c) Matthew: chapter 2, verses 1–23. Plan and script an imaginary radio or television programme which reports on the story of the wise men.

(d) What do you think the following aspects of the birth story of Jesus suggest the Gospel writers believed about the mission of Jesus?
   (i) He was born in very poor circumstances.
   (ii) He was visited by humble shepherds.
   (iii) He was visited by three very great men.

The Pilgrimage in Bethlehem

The most important place in Bethlehem for pilgrims to visit is the Church of the Nativity. A church was first built on this site in the early part of the fourth century CE. It was rebuilt in the sixth century and the church which the pilgrim visits today is basically that sixth century one, though of course, there have been alterations and additions since that time.

We asked Mr and Mrs Williams to tell us about their visit to this holy place. 'We were very excited indeed,' they said, 'as our coach climbed the hill into the town centre, we could already see the bell tower of the Church of the Nativity and immediately recalled hearing the sound of these bells on radio and television at Christmas time.'

Our question: Isn't the main town square called Manger Square?

Answer: Yes, that is correct. The coach parked in the square and we made our way across to the entrance of the church. The door, as you can see in our photograph, is very small indeed, and we had to stoop to enter. It is obvious that at one time it was a larger, arched door but part of it has been filled in to leave only this little entrance. We were told various reasons for the door being like this: some say that about 1500 CE. it was done to stop looters driving horses and wagons into the church; others say that it was to stop animals such as camels wandering in! Others again, looking for a more religious reason, say that it is to keep pilgrims humble as they enter this holy place, for they have to bow low to pass through it! Whatever the reason, certainly we felt humble as we entered the church built to commemorate the birth of Jesus so long ago.

Our question: Which branch of the Christian Church owns and looks after this Church of the Nativity?

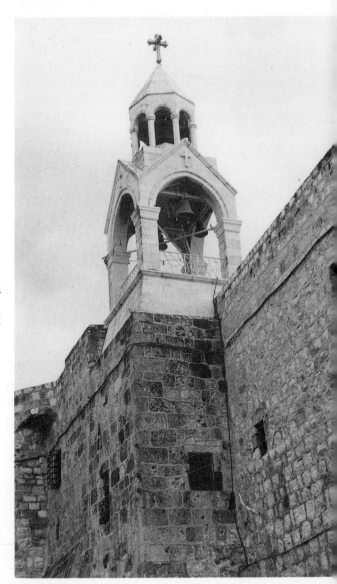

The Bell Tower

Entrance to the Church of the Nativity

Pilgrim at Shrine

Answer: As we entered, we were told that the part to the right of the high altar belonged to the Greek Orthodox Church and the part to the left belonged to the Armenian Church. Joined onto the building is a church belonging to Franciscan monks; it is known as the Church of St. Catherine. So you see that this important place of pilgrimage is actually owned and looked after by different groups of Christians. The Greek Orthodox priests all had beards and were dressed in long black robes; the Armenian priests had purple and cream coloured robes and the Franciscans wore simple brown habits. It was interesting to see the three different branches of the church each keeping to their own part of the building, and each worshipping in their own particular way.

Our question: Will you tell us of some of the sights you saw in the church which made it a memorable pilgrimage for you?

Answer: Well, in one part we came across a shrine which represented a manger and in it there was what looked like a doll representing the figure of the baby Jesus; above it was a picture of Mary, the mother of Jesus. We have to say that this shrine itself did not impress us very much, but what did impress us was the sight of pilgrims kneeling before it in prayer. It was obvious to us that their devotion was very real and that it meant a great deal to them to be praying quietly in this place.

To the left of the High Altar there is an area known as the Chapel of the Kings. This chapel is to commemorate the coming of the three kings, the so-called **Magi**, who, according to the story in Matthew's Gospel, came to visit the new-born child. As we stood there, we thought about that story and the gifts the kings were said to have brought – gold, frankincense and myrrh. We compared our comfortable journey by plane and coach, with their much harder journey, presumably by camel. They brought their gifts: what had we brought? In our hearts we told ourselves that we must live better lives as our gift to him.

Our question: Are we right in thinking that there is a star somewhere in the floor which marks the place where Jesus is thought to have been born?

Answer: Yes, that is right. We left the Chapel of the Kings and made our way down a flight of steps into the Grotto of the Nativity. Here we found ourselves in a cave, and it was not too difficult to imagine this as a stable behind the inn. The floor has been covered with white marble and in a corner is set a silver star with 14 points. Engraved on it are the words in Latin, *Hic de Virgine Maria Jesus Christus natus est* – 'Here Jesus Christ was born to the Virgin Mary'. Close by, on the north side of the cave, is what is believed to be the manger where the baby Jesus was laid.

Our question: What did you feel as you stood there in the grotto? Did you feel convinced that this really was the birthplace of Jesus?

Answer: Whether or not this was the true birthplace did not really matter to us. We were much more concerned about the important event which this place made us think about. Some pilgrims were clearly very moved indeed; some of them knelt down to kiss the star, others stood looking at it and we could see from the expressions on their faces that they were praying. Our own thoughts were of the Christian belief about the event commemorated here: that God cared so much about the world that he came, as a child born in such humble circumstances, sharing completely our kind of life. The word 'Incarnation' came to mind – God come among us in human flesh.

Our question: You have mentioned a chapel to remember the coming of the wise men; what about the shepherds? Is there any place you visited which made you think about that part of the birth story?

Answer: Yes, there is. Of course the exact spot where the shepherds had their vision is not known, but tradition points to two sites, both to the east of Bethlehem. One is where a Greek Orthodox Church is built inside a cave and it has been there since the fifth century

Star marking birth place

The shepherds' fields

49

CE. The other is not far from here and has a church belonging to the Franciscans built on it. For us, the best way of recollecting the vision of the shepherds was simply to stand on the edge of Bethlehem and look eastwards to the grassy slopes. It was not difficult to imagine shepherds sitting around a little fire, suddenly startled by a glorious vision of angels chanting 'Glory to God in the highest, and on earth peace among men with whom he is pleased!' As we stood there, we gave thanks to God for the coming of Jesus with his message of love and peace.

Task 2
List the sights at Bethlehem which you think would particularly help a Christian pilgrim to think about the birth of Jesus. Are there any aspects of the visit to Bethlehem which a Christian might find disappointing?

Task 3
One pilgrim said after a visit to the Church of the Nativity, 'I liked the dark cavern glittering with silver lamps, the gold, silver and tinsel ornaments, the smoky incense fumes, and the tapestried walls....' Another said, 'It would all have meant more to me if I had seen a bare cave which I could have imagined as a stable, without all the marble and the silver star....' Which of these two views would you support? Give your reasons.

Task 4
Write what you think would be an appropriate prayer for the pilgrim to be saying as she kneels before the shrine shown in the photograph on page 48.

Jerusalem

The other place of great importance to Christian pilgrims visiting the Holy Land is, of course, Jerusalem. Jesus must have known Jerusalem as a child; certainly we know he was in the city when he was 12 years old (see Luke: chapter 2, verses 41–51). After he began his preaching and teaching, he visited Jerusalem on a number of occasions, especially when a Jewish festival was being celebrated. The real importance of Jerusalem for the Christian, however, is that it was here that Jesus died and it was here that he rose from the dead, according to Christian belief.

The Pilgrimage Story
Jesus spent most of the three years of his 'public ministry' in Galilee, to the north of Israel. There came a day, however, when he set out for Jerusalem with his disciples. They, and many others, warned him against going because it was believed that his enemies in Jerusalem wanted to destroy him. Yet Jesus knew that he must go. When he reached Bethany, which is just outside the city, he borrowed a donkey and rode down the slopes of the Mount of Olives towards the city. Crowds gathered and shouted their welcome. Clearly the feeling in the crowd was that this was the Messiah, the one they believed God was sending to lead them into a new age of peace and prosperity.

He stopped on the slopes of the Mount and gazed over at the city; as he did so, he wept, saying, 'Would that even today, you knew the things that make for peace.' Somehow, he knew that in spite of the welcoming shouts, he would be rejected in the city.

When he reached the city, he went to the temple and caused a great stir by chasing out those who were selling animals for sacrifice. He told them that the temple was supposed to be a house of prayer, but they had made it a den of robbers!

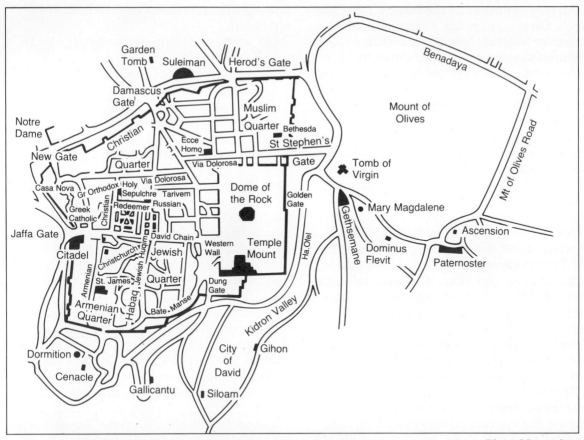

Plan of Jerusalem

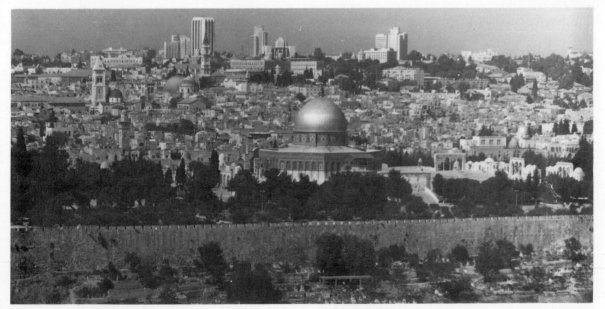

View from the Mount of Olives

51

All this happened at the beginning of the week. On the Thursday, since it was the Passover festival, Jesus met with his disciples to celebrate the Passover meal. Afterwards, they went out to the Garden of Gethsemane, at the foot of the Mount of Olives and there Jesus prayed that, if it was possible, he might be spared the suffering which lay ahead, for he knew that his enemies were about to act against him. Sure enough, while he was at prayer, they came to arrest him. He was taken before the Sanhedrin, the Chief Priest's court, and accused of speaking against God – the court called it 'blasphemy'. It was decided that he should die, but they would bring him before the Roman Governor, for he alone could order such an execution. The next morning, Pontius Pilate, the Governor, against his better judgement, agreed to the death sentence. Jesus was led away at about 9 o'clock on that Friday morning, to the place of execution, where he was nailed to a wooden cross and left to die.

By about 3 o'clock, it was all over; his body was taken down and laid in a tomb, with a stone rolled across the entrance. Early on Sunday morning, three women who went to the tomb found the stone rolled away and the tomb empty. Later they reported to the disciples that they had a vision in which they were told that Jesus had risen from the dead. Some time after, Jesus appeared to a number of his friends and gradually they were all convinced that he really had conquered death. He made various appearances to them over a period of about 40 days, then, on the Mount of Olives, he told them he must return to his Father, God; so he ascended to Heaven and left his followers to carry on all that he had begun.

Task 1

Many of the events in the last week of the life of Jesus were such that, if they happened today, they would be in the headlines! How do you think these events would be reported in our time? You will find the stories in the passages from Luke's Gospel which are set out below.

    (a) Jesus's entry to Jerusalem; Luke 19, v. 28–40.
    (b) In the temple; Luke 19, v. 45–48.
    (c) The Last Supper; Luke 22, v. 7–34.
    (d) His arrest; Luke 22, v. 39–71.
    (e) Trial before Pilate; Luke 23, v. 1–25.
    (f) The crucifixion; Luke 23, v. 26–56.
    (g) The resurrection; Luke 24, v. 1–53.

The Pilgrim in Jerusalem

Mr and Mrs Williams told us that they particularly wanted to try and relive the events in the last week of Jesus' life. They said, 'Although we visited many interesting places in the city, we also set aside time to try and follow, in order, the events of what we now often call Holy Week.'

Our question: That, no doubt, would mean starting at the top of the Mount of Olives?

Answer: Yes, that is correct. We made our way up to where the little village of Bethany had been and pictured the excited crowds when Jesus borrowed a donkey and began his ride to the city. It was not difficult to imagine the shouts, 'Hosanna! Blessed is he who comes in the name of the Lord!'

We walked along to the summit of the Mount of Olives, with its magnificent view of the old city. As we wended our way down the hillside we came to a beautiful little church called The Church of Dominus Flevit; *'dominus flevit'* is Latin, meaning 'the Lord wept'. As we sat in this church, we could see, through the window behind the altar, the old city. We thought of Jesus weeping for the city in his time and we recited together with fellow pilgrims the words of a prayer:

    Lord Jesus Christ,
    Today we share your tears for the cities of the world;
    Still we have not loved the things that make for peace.
    We weep for the divided cities:
    Where brother fights with brother,
    Where anger feeds on hatred,

Where prejudice blinds the eyes of
compassion.
We weep for our cities and for
ourselves;
We have not learned the things that
make for peace.
Lord, turn tears to love,
And love to work.
Turn work to justice,
And all that makes for peace.

We carried on past the Garden of
Gethsemane to which we would return later,
across the narrow Kidron Valley and up into
the city, through St. Stephen's Gate. Jesus
probably would have entered by the Golden
Gate, but it has been bricked up since the
time of the Crusades. We made our way onto
the Temple Mount which is now a holy place
for Muslims, with the magnificent Mosque of
Omar 'the Dome of the Rock'. In Jesus' time,

of course, the Jewish Temple, long since
destroyed, stood here. Our thoughts here
were of Jesus striding into the temple
courtyard after his triumphant ride to the
city. Blazing with anger he showed his
passion for justice as he chased out those who
were exploiting the pilgrims who had come
to worship.
Our question: What about a prayer at this
place?
Answer: Yes, our prayer here was a simple
one: 'Lord, give us the courage to stand out
against evil when we see it rather than
taking the easy way of looking in the other
direction.'
Our question: These are the events at the
beginning of Holy Week: where did your
pilgrimage take you from there?
Answer: We move now to the Thursday, the
day of the Last Supper. No one is sure where
exactly this took place but inevitably, earlier

View looking at the Mount of Olives

The Garden of Gethsemane

Christians wanted somewhere to commemorate this important event. This place is known as the **Cenacle**; it is a large upper room, reached by a steep, narrow flight of stairs. It is just a large, empty room, with the roof supported by ornate pillars and certainly is no older than the fourteenth century CE.

Our question: So, it was not really worth going there, since it had no direct connection with Jesus?

Answer: No! We would not say that! You see, for us the event remembered there was more important than the place itself.

Certainly, this seemed much too grand a place: we imagined the upper room of the Last Supper as a much smaller place – probably the upstairs room in a very humble home. Nevertheless, standing in this place one could picture a long table, with Jesus and the 12 disciples reclining around it, as was the custom. We could imagine the puzzled expressions on the disciples' faces as he talked about the bread being his body broken for them, and the wine as his blood shed for them; at this stage, they could not really understand what he meant.

Other memories which came to us were that Judas left the Last Supper to betray Jesus to his enemies, and that Jesus told Peter that before the cock crowed three times, he would deny knowing him. Remembering these incidents, we prayed, 'Lord, as we try to follow you, give us the courage never to betray or deny you, but to be your faithful followers, all our days.' It would have been a great experience for us if we could have celebrated Holy Communion in this place, but we were told that no such services were allowed. As we left to go across to the Garden of Gethsemane we were very conscious of how Jesus must have felt as he made his way there, knowing that before the evening was over, he would be arrested.

Our question: Do you think the Garden of Gethsemane, as it is now, is the actual place where Jesus went in his lifetime?

Answer: Yes, it must have been around this spot. No doubt it all looked rather different in those days, but there are still very old olive trees, and it is a pleasant, quiet spot. Now there is a fine church by the garden – it is called the Church of the Agony, because here, Jesus agonised in prayer, asking God to spare him the ordeal which lay ahead. Then he became calmer and said, 'Not my will, but yours be done!'

Our question: Is it not sometimes referred to as the Church of All Nations?

Answer: Yes, that is correct. When it was built in 1924, many nations contributed to the cost. We prefer to remember it as the

Church of the Agony

Jesus at prayer

Church of the Agony, because of what happened here. This church, of course, is built over a much earlier one and the altar stands behind a large square of rough rock, believed to be where Jesus prayed. While we were there, a service for pilgrims was in progress. It became for us then a Church of All Nations, because so many nationalities were present that day; a group of German pilgrims burst into a song of praise to Christ and we found it all very moving indeed.

Out in the garden we came across two simple but very memorable sculptures: one portrays Jesus at prayer, the other shows him being arrested and led away by his enemies. We stood in front of each of these for some time, quietly thinking of what happened at this holy place – Jesus feeling so desperately alone, as he thought of what lay ahead, the tired disciples dozing off to sleep and Jesus saying to them, 'Could you not stay awake with me one hour?' We found ourselves condemning them – how could they sleep at such a time? Then we were reminded of part of a meditation we had read before coming on this pilgrimage:

> 'Lord, the sleep of the disciples falls on our unwilling eyes too;
> We often sleep while you agonise over the hungry of the world.
> We sleep while you long for your suffering children to be helped and comforted.'
> And so we prayed, 'Lord, keep us awake and alive to your needs which we can help to meet in today's world.'

Task 2

At the site marked by the Church of Dominus Flevit, Jesus wept and said, 'Would that you knew the things that make for peace.' What things in today's society might have made him weep, and what things might he have in mind that make for peace?

Task 3

In what ways might Christian pilgrims be helped by visiting places especially associated with the last week of Jesus' life?

The Arrest

56

The Via Dolorosa

As the pilgrims made their way once more across the narrow Kidron Valley and up into the old city, Mr Williams said they tried to imagine themselves as part of that sad procession as Jesus was led to the house of the High Priest.

Our question: Is this the point at which you began to follow the traditional pilgrim's way of the Via Dolorosa?

Answer: Yes, once we were in the narrow streets of the old city we followed the 'way of the Cross', the **Via Dolorosa**, which has been followed by Christian pilgrims for centuries. It is marked by 14 so-called **Stations of the Cross**, i.e. places which mark events involving Jesus on his way to the place of crucifixion.

Our question: Do all these stations relate to incidents mentioned in the Bible?

Pilgrims on the Via Dolorosa

Answer: No! Five of them do not, but depend rather on traditions which have been passed down; these are the third, fourth, sixth, seventh and ninth – but let us tell you briefly about each of the stations. The first is the traditional place where the Roman fortress stood and it is thought that here Jesus was brought before Pontius Pilate and condemned. Now it is the playground of a Palestinian school! The second is under an arch on the Via Dolorosa, known as the Ecce Homo Arch. Here pilgrims remember Jesus being given the cross to carry.

The third station is outside a small chapel and marks the spot where tradition says Jesus fell for the first time under the weight of the cross.

The fourth station is by another little chapel and here the tradition is that Jesus met his mother as he carried the cross. The fifth is to remind pilgrims of the place where the soldiers forced a man, Simon from Cyrene, to carry the cross for Jesus.

The sixth is at a simple chapel where a woman, Veronica, is said to have wiped the sweat from the face of Jesus; the story continues that the handkerchief was permanently imprinted with the true image of his face.

The seventh is marked by a pillar which recalls Jesus' second fall as he stumbled on his way to crucifixion.

The eighth station is marked by a small cross engraved on the wall, with words in Greek which mean, 'Jesus Christ is the Victor'. This is to commemorate Jesus telling the women of Jerusalem, as they followed the sad procession, that they should not weep for him.

The ninth is at the entrance to a church looked after by Ethiopian monks. This keeps alive the tradition that, once again, Jesus fell.

The rest of the stations are at the Church of the Holy Sepulchre. This is, for many Christians, the most holy place to which they can ever come. It is divided between six different Christian communities, so there are many different kinds of chapels inside.

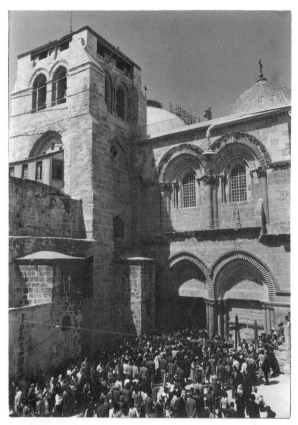

Pilgrims entering Church of Holy Sepulchre

Mosaic in the Latin Chapel

The tenth station is observed either in the square outside the church, or just inside the door; this reminds pilgrims of Jesus being stripped of his garments before being put on the cross.

The eleventh is reached by climbing stairs inside the church to where there are two little chapels. The first is known as the Latin Chapel of Calvary. Here pilgrims think of Jesus being nailed to the cross. There is a mosaic on the wall which depicts that scene. Adjoining is the Greek Orthodox Chapel of Calvary which marks the twelfth station: here is the traditional scene of the crucifixion.

The thirteenth station is found by going down the stairs again, to where there is a slab of marble, decorated with lamps hanging from the canopy above it. Some Christians commemorate the anointing of Jesus' body at this place.

The final station of the Cross is at the Holy Sepulchre itself; this is like a little stone house in the middle of the church. It covers a tomb which the builders of the church, centuries ago, had carefully preserved from the rock which surrounded it. Here, many believe, is the tomb in which the body of Jesus was laid.

Our question: It must have been a fascinating walk past these holy places. Before telling us your memories of visiting some of them, will you give us a general impression of the route? No doubt the narrow streets are busy; does that not make it difficult to think of Jesus and what happened to him here so long ago?

Answer: No, not at all! In fact it almost made it easier because, of course, these same streets would have been busy then too. As that sad procession passed along, there would have been jostling crowds, the selling of wares, laughing and shouting, just as there was when we followed the route. It was much more than a fascinating walk: it was a spiritual experience which we will never forget.

Our question: Do any of these stations of the cross stand out in your memory as highlights of your pilgrimage?

Answer: We talked together about this afterwards and came to the conclusion that none of them did! It was the whole experience of walking the Via Dolorosa and reflecting on the last experiences of Jesus as he was led to his death, which made it all such an important pilgrimage. If we were being completely honest we would have to say that the Church of the Holy Sepulchre did not impress us very much at all: the shrines of Calvary did not really speak to us of the stark scene we had in our minds from reading the Gospel accounts of the crucifixion. What did impress us, however, was the devotion of fellow pilgrims – it was them and their prayers which made all this so special. We offered prayers at each of the stations, but the thoughts and the prayer which we remember most were at the shrine of Calvary. We thought especially of Jesus' prayer on the cross 'Father, forgive them for they don't know what they are doing'. We read the words of a meditation:

'Lord, to your disciples, that day at Calvary must have seemed all darkness and defeat: did it seem like that to you? Your hands, carpenter's hands, hands that touched the leper and blessed the child, were twisted and splintered as they drove in the nails. Your body, the temple of God, they stripped and stretched out like a bow. Did you long to protest your innocence? To cry out for justice....?'

The Greek Orthodox Chapel

The Holy Sepulchre (*above*) and The Garden Tomb (*below*)

Our prayer was, 'Jesus, as you could find it in your heart to forgive those who were the cause of your suffering, those who were taking your life from you, help us to forgive each other for the wrongs done to us. Forgive us, too, for often we do not know what we do that offends you. May we be reassured that you tell us to go in peace, for our sins have been forgiven.'

Our question: Surely visiting the sepulchre itself must have been a highlight of your pilgrimage? After all, isn't the resurrection of Jesus one of the most important aspects of the Christian faith?

Answer: Of course it is! And visiting the sepulchre reminded us very forcibly of the resurrection. But there were two other places we visited on our pilgrimage which made us reflect even more about the resurrection, and the memories of these places are most vivid in our minds. One of these is the Garden Tomb, which is a lovely spot outside the present walls of the old city. In the garden is a tomb cut out of the rock, with an entrance which would have been closed by rolling a large stone across it. This tomb certainly dates back to at least the first century CE. The British General Charles Gordon was in Jerusalem in 1883 when he saw, not far from the Damascus Gate, a little hill which seemed to him to look like the shape of a skull. He immediately believed he had found the place where Jesus had been crucified, for it was called 'the place of the skull'. Since he also discovered that close to it lay this ancient tomb, he was even more convinced that he had found both the place of execution and the tomb of Jesus.

Our question: You believe then, that this was the actual tomb, since you say visiting here was more memorable than the Holy Sepulchre?

Answer: No! I am sure the Church of the Holy Sepulchre is much more likely to be the area where it all took place, but to stand quietly at the Garden Tomb is an experience never to be forgotten, for the scene is so simple and fits the image one has always had in mind of the burial place. Someone told us before our visit, 'It is easier to pray at the Garden Tomb than it is at the Holy Sepulchre'; we certainly found that to be true as we stood gazing at the empty tomb and thought quietly of Christ's victory over evil and death.

The other place associated with the resurrection of Jesus which is most memorable to us is in Galilee. As part of our pilgrimage we visited Galilee, which is in the north of Israel. Here Jesus spent most of the three years when he went around preaching and teaching. Close to the remains of Capernaum, a little town which was most familiar to him, there is a beautiful little church known as the Church of St. Peter, or 'the Chapel of the Primacy'.

It is built on a rock which juts into the Sea of Galilee. Here, it is thought, the risen Jesus appeared to the disciples, and especially to Peter. As we stood outside this place, with the sound of the water lapping at the edge of the lake, one pilgrim read aloud the words from the Gospel According to St. John, chapter 21 verses 4–17, which tell of the risen Jesus appearing and talking to Peter. We then sang together a song of praise about the resurrection. Again, here, it was much easier to visualise the scene beside the peaceful lake, and it was certainly easier to pray here.

Now that we are home and look back on our pilgrimage, we find that we are not just left with memories: the experiences of visiting and praying at these holy places have strengthened our faith and made us more determined to be better Christians. Certainly the pilgrimage for us was 'a journey of a lifetime', a truly spiritual experience.

The Chapel of the Primacy

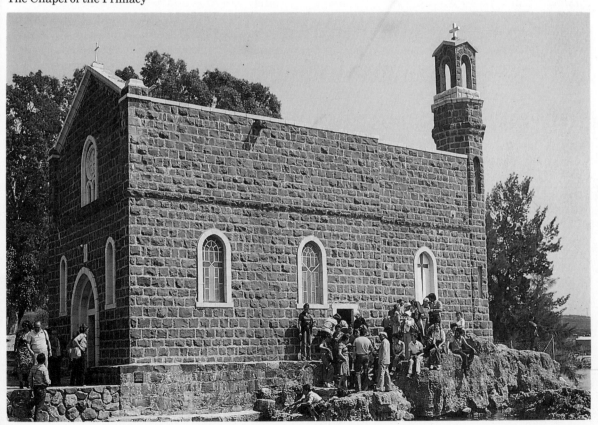

Task 4
Write the heading in your book, 'The Stations of the Cross'; make three columns underneath labelled: Station; 'What or where it is'; 'What it commemorates'. Fill in the detail for all 14 stations.

Task 5
Bearing in mind what Christians believe about Jesus, which Stations of the Cross do you think pilgrims would regard as more important than others? Give reasons for your answer.

Task 6
Produce a leaflet which a tourist agent might use to attract Christians to go on pilgrimage to Jerusalem. Include as much detail as you can which you think will be of interest to Christians.

Task 7
The pilgrims found it easier to pray at the Garden Tomb than at the Church of the Holy Sepulchre. Write a paragraph in which you show either that (a) you understand why this was, or (b) that you are surprised by this.

Task 8
Read in your Bible John: chapter 21, verses 4–17.
  (a) Bearing in mind that Peter had earlier denied knowing Jesus what would this incident have meant to him?
  (b) What might Christian pilgrims, standing beside the place where it almost certainly took place, find in the incident which challenges them to be better Christians.

Task 9
In a hymn book used in your school assembly see if you can find hymns which would have been appropriate for pilgrims to sing at the Garden of Gethsemane, the Chapel of Calvary and the Holy Sepulchre.

Lourdes

Map showing position of Lourdes

The French town of Lourdes lies at the foot of the Pyrenees, the mountain range which separates France from Spain. Lourdes attracts many thousands of Christian pilgrims every year, especially a large number who are sick or handicapped in some way. Many sick folk have been greatly helped by their visit, or even completely cured of some illness. Lourdes is a place of great happiness; pilgrims who travel here say that they cannot be in Lourdes for many days without being inspired to help others less fortunate than themselves. Even sick pilgrims who do not find physical healing say that their faith has been strengthened, and they return from Lourdes with a different attitude towards their illness.

The Pilgrimage Story
Bernadette Soubirous was born in Lourdes on 7 January 1844. Her father was a miller, but soon after her birth, he experienced serious financial difficulties and the family became very poor indeed.

On 11 February 1858, when Bernadette was 14 years old, she was out with her sister and a friend collecting firewood. They had wandered down the river bank to a spot known as Massabielle where there was a cave. Here Bernadette heard a noise like a gust of wind and when she looked up at the cave, she saw a lady standing in a niche just above the cave entrance. The lady was dressed in white, with a blue sash round her waist and she had a rosary over her arm. Bernadette felt that the figure was inviting her to kneel down and pray. Her sister and friend had wandered off, looking for firewood, and when they returned, they found Bernadette kneeling and gazing up at the niche. She told them of her vision, but they only laughed and said she must have been dreaming. When she told her mother of this strange experience, she too thought it was her imagination and told her to stay away from the cave.

Bernadette, however, three days later, persuaded her parents to let her visit the spot again; as she prayed there, the lady appeared once more. On her third visit, the figure not only appeared to her but also spoke, asking if Bernadette would come every day for a fortnight. She also said, 'I do not promise to make you happy in this life, but in the next!'

Obviously, in a small community like Lourdes, interest was aroused in what had happened, for Bernadette made no secret of her visions. People began to follow her to the cave but no one else shared any of the visions with her. Thursday 25 February was an important day, for on that day Bernadette was told by the lady to drink and wash in the water from the spring at the cave. Bernadette had to scratch in the ground, for there was little water. Before the day was ended, what had at first been a tiny trickle became a stream pouring out into the river.

On 2 March, the lady appeared to the young girl for the thirteenth time. She told her to ask the priest at Lourdes to build a chapel at the cave and to have regular processions there. The priest at this stage, however, did not believe Bernadette's visions, and shared the view held by many

that it was all happening in her imagination.

At a later appearance of the lady, Bernadette asked her name. She replied, 'I am the Immaculate Conception! I want a chapel built here!' The doctrine of 'the Immaculate Conception of the Blessed Virgin Mary' had only been formally set down by the Pope four years before Bernadette's visions. Basically, it is the belief that since Mary gave birth to Jesus, she must have been such a special person that even before her birth, she was free from all stain of sins. Bernadette, who had little or no education, knew nothing of this doctrine; the words 'Immaculate Conception' meant nothing to her. However, they were

Pilgrims at Lourdes

understood by the priest; indeed, the naming of the lady in this way went a long way towards convincing him that Bernadette was telling the truth.

In all, the lady appeared to Bernadette 18 times, the last time being on 16 July. Life became difficult for Bernadette after this, for such interest had been aroused by her experiences that curious visitors from near and far came to both the cave and her home. She was questioned by the police and the civil authorities who did not believe what she told them. Fortunately, by now the priest was convinced of her sincerity, and the result was that the Bishop of Lourdes set up a commission to investigate the whole matter.

After two years, the commission reported that they believed she was telling the truth; the Virgin Mary had in fact appeared to Bernadette.

In 1864 a marble statue of the lady was set up in the niche above the cave; it was based on the description given to the sculptor by Bernadette.

Bernadette eventually became a nun in the convent at Nevers in central France. She experienced great sadness and suffering, and her account of her visions was often misunderstood. She compared herself to a broom and used to say, 'Our Lady used me then put me back in my corner! I am happy there and there I stay!'

She died an early death in 1879 at the age of 35. Three years before her death a church was built and consecrated on a site just above the cave; so the lady's request to Bernadette was fulfilled. Even before the building of the church, people had begun to make pilgrimages to this place and some had even claimed to be healed of illnesses. Pilgrimages, and also some healings, continue to this day.

Task 1
Set down in a column the important dates in the story of Bernadette. Opposite each date briefly state what the event was.

Task 2
Imagine you are the sister of Bernadette. Tell Bernadette's story from her sister's point of view.

Task 3
People in Lourdes were divided about whether or not to believe the story of Bernadette. Imagine an argument between those who believe and those who do not.

On Pilgrimage at Lourdes
'The happiest week of my life!' That was the comment made by Sarah, a young handicapped girl from our community. Sarah went on pilgrimage to Lourdes with a group from one of the local churches. The party included a number of handicapped and sick people, as well as some who were in good health. We asked Sarah to tell us first of all about her arrival at Lourdes. She told us, 'We flew to France from Birmingham Airport and a special coach took us to Hosanna House, where we were to stay in Lourdes. Hosanna House belongs to the Handicapped Children's Pilgrimage Trust, an organisation which helps to make it possible for people like me to go on pilgrimage. It was a wonderful place to stay; we felt very tired after the journey and we were excited at coming to Lourdes, but everyone was so friendly and kind to us and soon we felt very much at home.'
Our question: We believe there are three churches built high above the grotto where Bernadette's visions took place. Presumably you visited at least one of these?
Answer: Yes, there are three churches which are linked together – the Crypt, the Rosary Church and the large Basilica of the Immaculate Conception. In the morning, we were taken to the Rosary Church for Mass which was celebrated by our own priest who had come with our party. It was a thrilling experience to be given the Sacrament, in this place which had been built because Our Lady, who appeared in a vision to Bernadette, asked for it to be built! After

Mass, we were taken to experience something very different – a visit to the baths. These too, we feel are holy, for they remind us of Our Lady's command to Bernadette to go and wash in the spring from the grotto.

Our question: So the water at the baths comes from the grotto spring?

Answer: Oh Yes! The baths have been built to make it easier for pilgrims, especially those like me who are handicapped, to bathe in the water. There are always many skilled helpers there, and they assisted us. I was helped into a kind of harness and four helpers took a corner each and lowered me into the water. It was very cold, but that did not seem to worry me, for I was thinking of where I was and all that is associated with it. One thing which struck me as strange was that no one needed to be dried! There were no towels; everyone dressed while still wet and in a few minutes were all warm and dry!

Our question: Didn't the Lady also say that the water was to be drunk? Surely you didn't drink the water at the bath?

Candles and the Altar (from behind Altar)

The Statue

The Grotto

Answer: Yes she did say 'drink the water'; in fact she never asked that people bathe in it, but that custom developed soon after pilgrimages began. We drank the water at the next stage of our pilgrimage. By the grotto there are rows of taps from which water from the spring can be drawn. Here we were given some of the cool, clear water to drink.

Our question: Tell us of your impressions of the grotto. This must be a very important part of the pilgrimage since this is where the visions took place.

Answer: Yes, indeed it is, and my visit there will always live in my memory. Our party stood looking into the grotto; I and others like me, of course, were in our wheelchairs. In the centre of the entrance to the cave was a plain, stone altar with a very simple crucifix; to one side was a large stand with many candles burning. These had been placed there and lit by pilgrims as they prayed for their friends, especially those who were ill. Above the grotto was the niche where the lady had appeared. In it is the marble statue of Our Lady, with the words she spoke to Bernadette in the local dialect of the time, *'que soy era Immaculada Councepciou'* – 'I am the Immaculate Conception'. Everything was quiet: the only sounds were the murmured prayers of fellow pilgrims and the pleasant gurgling of the spring water from within the cave. There were signs here and there reminding pilgrims to keep quiet. All this helped to give a strong feeling of worship and devotion.

Pilgrims gathering for the procession

Our question: What did you feel in general about the grotto?

Answer: I certainly felt it was a very holy place indeed; there was an atmosphere about it which cannot really be described. There was no doubt in my mind that something miraculous had taken place here, and it was made even more sacred by the knowledge that for about 130 years, pilgrims have been coming here to pray.

Our question: The Lady also told Bernadette that she wanted processions to be held here. Does this happen, and if so, what kind of processions are there?

Answer: Every afternoon there is a procession of pilgrims from the grotto led by the Bishop bearing the Blessed Sacrament.

Our question: Will you explain what is meant by 'the Blessed Sacrament'?

Answer: The **Blessed Sacrament** is the wafer of unleavened bread consecrated in the Mass, and is the Body of Christ. It has been placed in a **monstrance**, a transparent container, and the Bishop holds this aloft so that everyone can see it. The procession moves into the huge Rosary Square in front of the Basilica where the sick lie waiting: I was among them. The Bishop blessed each one of us by holding the monstrance above us; many of the sick pilgrims murmured prayers such as, 'Lord, that I may walk!', 'Lord, that I may see!', 'Lord, thy will be done!'; others were saying, 'Praise the Lord, all peoples of the earth!'

In the evening there is another procession which is a very happy affair. I was able to take part in it as my handicap does not really make me ill. As I was pushed along in my wheelchair, I was part of a vast crowd, all of whom carried lighted candles. The whole crowd was singing and the sound must have been heard through the whole district. Even those who were too sick to join the procession felt part of it, for in the hospital wards where they were staying, the doctors and nurses had a procession round the wards and each of the patients held a candle and joined in the singing.

There is one part of the pilgrimage which I must share with you. In the woods on the hillside above the grotto a 'Way of the Cross' has been made. At intervals along the route, the 14 Stations of the Cross have been placed. Each of these is marked by a group of life-size, bronze figures which reminds of the 14

Bishop with the sick

The Way of the Cross

stages of Christ's journey to the cross. The path is quite rough and, while I was pushed in my chair with some difficulty, some pilgrims walked it barefoot. This was their way of sharing in the sufferings of Christ and showing their sorrow for their sins.

Our question: You have certainly convinced us that your pilgrimage was a wonderful experience; perhaps you will answer one more question. You are still in a wheelchair, so your visit to Lourdes did not bring you healing, and yet you say it was the happiest week of your life! Can you explain why?

Answer: It would, of course, have been wonderful if I had been cured, but that was not really uppermost in my mind. My faith in God was made stronger by my pilgrimage – *and* my faith in my fellow human beings, because I have never experienced such an atmosphere of love and care and concern at any other time in my life. Also, I came to realise that my handicap is nothing compared with the suffering of others whom I saw at Lourdes; I came away thankful for what I am able to do in spite of my handicap. Truly, it was and always will be, the happiest week of my life!'

We felt we must ask some of the able bodied pilgrims what their experience of Lourdes was; they told us the same story. One said, 'The feeling that people cared about each other was stronger here than I have ever experienced anywhere else! If you were not pushing a wheelchair, taking the arm of someone who was lame, or in some way helping people who needed assistance, you felt out of place, as if you had no right to be in Lourdes!'

We had one final question to put to the group of pilgrims:

Our question: This pilgrimage seems to be more in honour of the Virgin Mary than it is of Jesus, and yet Jesus is surely more important to you as Christians?

Answer: Of course Jesus is most important to us, but here, we believe, Bernadette had a vision of the Blessed Virgin Mary and that experience strengthened her faith in Jesus.

We believe that by coming here and by honouring Mary, we are also honouring her son, Jesus. His message was always one of love and caring concern for others. Our experience of Lourdes has made us return home more determined to live our lives in the way that Jesus said we should.

Task 4
Make up a table which lists the places visited by the handicapped pilgrim to Lourdes. Against each one write a brief paragraph explaining what was special about that place.

Task 5
Explain the following terms used in the pilgrim's story:
  (a) the Mass
  (b) a crucifix
  (c) a rosary
  (d) the Blessed Sacrament
  (e) a monstrance
  (f) the Stations of the Cross.

Task 6
What do you think would be the most memorable experience of a pilgrim at Lourdes? Give reasons for your answer.

Task 7
Plan a leaflet which gives information to people interested in going on pilgrimage to Lourdes. It should be designed to make the pilgrimage as attractive as possible.

4 Muslim Pilgrimages

General view of Mecca

The Hajj

In the city of Mecca, in Saudi Arabia, there stands a simple building called the **Kaaba**, in the centre of the city's sacred mosque. Five times every day, Muslims all over the world face in the direction of this building as they offer their prayers to Allah. Each year, over two million Muslims travel to Mecca in order to fulfil the command given in the **Qur'an**, the Muslim's holy book, that every Muslim shall aim, at least once in a lifetime, to make this pilgrimage which is known as the **Hajj**. Muslims may make the journey to visit

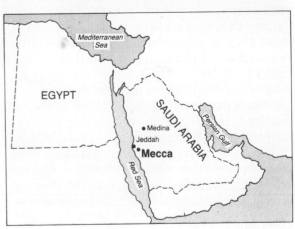

Map of Saudi Arabia

Mecca and the various holy places at any time of the year; such a visit is known as **Umrah** or 'the Lesser Pilgrimage'. The Hajj, the true pilgrimage, can only be made during the twelfth month in the Muslim calendar, **Dhu-el-Hijja**.

The Pilgrimage Story

To understand why Mecca is so important to Muslims we have to go back to the time of Abraham. The Jews consider Abraham to be their great ancestor and he is sometimes referred to as 'the Father of the Hebrew People'. Muslims also, however, regard him as their great ancestor; while the Jewish people trace their ancestry back to Abraham through his son Isaac, Muslims trace the ancestry of the Arab peoples to him through his son, Ishmael.

The Qur'an describes Abraham as 'the Friend of Allah' and tells of his concern that people worshipped idols of stone which they had made themselves. Abraham rejected stone idols as gods; he thought perhaps the stars, the moon or the sun might be God. In the end he came to believe that God was the unseen but ever-present one.

Abraham was married to Sarah, but they had no children, so, with Sarah's permission, he also married Hagar, his wife's slave girl. She gave birth to Ishmael, but Sarah became very jealous. When Ishmael was still only an infant, Abraham believed that God wanted him to go to Mecca and to leave Hagar and Ishmael there. The story tells how he saw a sandy hill, under which was hidden the ruins of a house of God built by Adam. Near to this hill, he left Hagar and Ishmael with only a bag of dates and a skin full of water. According to Muslim tradition, when Hagar realised that Abraham was leaving her because of God's command, she said, 'Allah will not let us die!' After Abraham had gone and she became parched with thirst, she ran to the nearby hill looking for water; finding none, she ran to the other hill she could see, but again found no water. She ran between the hills seven times calling on Allah to help

her, then to her great relief and joy she saw a spring pouring forth water near where her son was lying. This place, where she settled with her son, she called Zamzam and the two hills became known as Safa and Marwa.

Again according to Muslim tradition, years later, Abraham believed that God wanted him to sacrifice his most precious possession. As he still loved Ishmael dearly, he came to believe that God was telling him to offer his son as a sacrifice! He was about to carry out this dreadful act when God spoke to him telling him he had proved his willingness to obey. Just then, he saw a large ram running down the hill to nearby Mina. He chased and caught it offering it as a sacrifice to God, thankful that he had not killed his own dear son.

Years later, when Hagar had died, Abraham asked Ishmael to help him build a house for Allah. They discovered the ruins of the one built by Adam and so they laid new foundations and built a house of stone: it was dedicated to the worship of Allah by circling it seven times. This was the first Kaaba built on this already sacred spot in Mecca. The time when all this took place was about the year 2000 BCE.

To continue the story we have to leap forward to the year 571 CE when Muhammad was born in Mecca. By the time he was 35 years old, Muhammad had become a well-respected member of the community. About this time, the Kaaba was badly in need of rebuilding and the four Arab tribes represented in Mecca shared the task.

This rebuilding of the Kaaba, however, was not to make it the kind of House of God which Abraham had made it. It was in fact the house of many idols, which the Arab tribes had worshipped for a very long time. Muhammad became increasingly troubled about this and, like Abraham centuries before, considered how futile and meaningless idol worship really was. When he was 40 years old he began to have visions: messages from God given in these visions were written down and these form the

Qur'an, the Muslim's holy book.

Muhammad tried for about 13 years to share his message with the people of Mecca but the converts among them were comparatively few. However, he found considerable support from the people of Yathrib, a city some 300 miles to the north. In 622 CE, therefore, when there was a serious plot in Mecca to kill him, he left secretly and settled in Yathrib, a city which later took the name Madinat-ar-Rasul, i.e. 'the City of the Prophet'; it is more commonly known as Medina. Here the new religion of Islam made great progress and the faith spread beyond Medina itself. Eight years later Muhammad and his followers were able to advance on Mecca and capture the city. He assured the Meccan people that he forgave them for their previous opposition to his message and he had the Kaaba cleared of all idols and anything which had to do with idol worship. From now on, the Kaaba was to be dedicated to the worship of the one God. Arab pilgrims had previously come here to worship the idols which inhabited this shrine; now they would come to worship the one God, Allah, who had revealed himself through the earlier prophets like Abraham and finally through the prophet Muhammad.

Task 1
Write down what you understand by the following:
  (a) Umrah
  (b) Dhu-el-Hijja
  (c) Yathrib.

Task 2
What do Muslims believe about:
  (a) Abraham
  (b) the Kaaba?

Task 3
Why are the following places important on the Hajj:
  (a) the Kaaba
  (b) Zamzam
  (c) Safa and Marwa?

Task 4
Once, when a festival was being celebrated, Abraham smashed all the idols, except one, the biggest of them all, The people were very angry and afraid and suspected that Abraham had done this terrible deed. When they challenged him, he said, 'Ask the biggest idol who did it!'

'You know,' they replied, 'that idols cannot speak!' 'Then why do you worship them,' said Abraham, 'when they cannot move or do anything?'

Make this incident into a short story to include:
  (a) what you think was said when the people discovered the destruction of the idols;
  (b) the conversation between them and Abraham;
  (c) what you think the people's reaction was to what Abraham said.

Making the Pilgrimage
Non-Muslims are not allowed to visit Mecca; any Muslim from another country like Britain must obtain a 'pilgrimage visa' from the Saudi Arabian Consulate and must prove that he or she really is a member of the Muslim community. The reason given for this is that Islam is a complete way of life which involves all daily activities. Mecca gives a unique opportunity to Muslims to live their faith without being influenced in any way by other religious beliefs and practices.

We talked to Mr and Mrs Ahmad, who live in our community, about the time when they made the Hajj. The first part of our conversation was as follows.

Our question: Before you tell us about your visit to Mecca, can you satisfy our curiosity about the command that every Muslim should make the Hajj once in a lifetime? It must be very difficult for some Muslims to obey this, if they live a long way from Mecca, as you do, and if they only have a limited income. Do you believe Allah expects such people to make the journey?

Answer: No! Not at all! If by spending money

to make the Hajj we had deprived our family, it would have been quite wrong for us to go. The Holy Qur'an states that it is only a duty for those who can afford to go. It is also made clear that we should be in good health, and should not be risking our lives by going if we are ill.

Mr and Mrs Ahmad told us of their preparations for the Hajj. Mr Ahmad had packed two white sheets among his clothes which he would wear on the pilgrimage. One

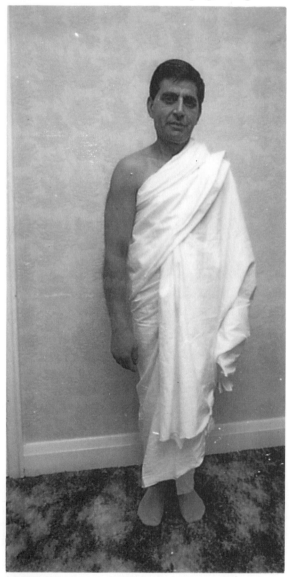

Muslim in pilgrim's dress

would be wrapped around the lower part of his body and the other would be loosely thrown over his shoulder. He explained that all men on the Hajj would be dressed like this to emphasise that all are equal. Mrs Ahmad packed a simple, long dress which she would wear, she also made sure that she had a white scarf because it is important for women to cover the head on the Hajj.

One thing which they had found especially moving was that many of their Muslim friends and acquaintances begged them to pray for them when they were at the holy places. This made them feel how privileged they were to be able to fulfil their duty to make the Hajj.

They set out for us some of the rituals and rules to be observed on the Hajj, which you can see in the table. We asked them when they began to observe these rules. They replied that they put on **ihram** at Gatwick Airport where rooms had been set aside for pilgrims to wash and change their clothes. They put on the pilgrimage garments here, because during the flight they might pass over the sacred area of Mecca. In fact, they told us that the plane did fly over Mecca and the pilot announced this well in advance so that any pilgrims who had not already changed could do so in the aircraft toilets. Since the ritual washing known as **wudu** has to be performed before changing, it was much easier to do this before joining the aircraft.

Task 5
    (a) Draw a pilgrim, showing the pilgrimage dress.
    (b) Explain simply what the pilgrim must do to enter a state of ihram.
    (c) Write out a list of things which are forbidden to the pilgrim. Against each one write a brief explanation of its significance.
    (d) How might observing these rules help the pilgrim to make Hajj in a right spirit? Do you think it is good idea to have such rules?

Rituals and rules to be observed when going on Hajj

Before entering the area in which Mecca is situated, the pilgrim must:

1 Take a bath.

This symbolises purity.

2 Put on the pilgrimage dress as follows:

Men: two sheets of unsewn, white material
Women: a clean, plain dress

This symbolises the equality of all Muslims. It also reminds the pilgrims that they are humble servants of Allah and are turning their backs on pride and vanity. It is said to be a reminder that this life is not all that is important; death will come, the body will be wrapped in white sheets and all the luxuries of this life will be left behind.

When these rules have been carried out, the pilgrim is said to have entered a state of **ihram**, He or she must remain in this state of ihram for the whole of the Hajj, by observing the following rules.

1 No perfume of any kind may be used.

This is to help the pilgrim forget the luxuries of everyday life.

2 No animals or even insects should be killed or harmed.

This is a reminder that everything belongs to Allah, the Creator.

3 No plants should be uprooted or damaged.

This is to foster a love for the world of nature which is Allah's creation.

4 Nothing dishonest or unkind should be done.

This is to aim at being a true servant of Allah.

5 No weapon should be carried.

This is to symbolise the giving up of any spirit of aggression.

6 The head must be covered.

This is an expression of humility.

7 Hair and nails should not be cut while in the state of ihram.

This is to express non-interference with nature.

8 No sexual intercourse.

This is to forget worldly pleasure and concentrate on the spiritual.

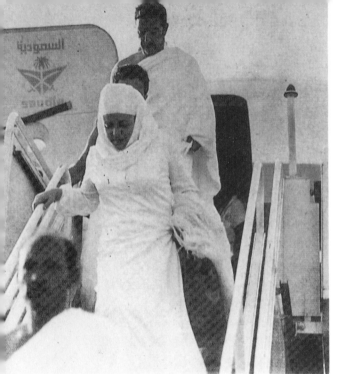

Pilgrims leaving plane

Mecca

The aircraft landed at Jeddah, which is the main airport for Saudi Arabia. Here Mr and Mrs Ahmad and the rest of their group were met by a **mutawwif** or pilgrim's guide, with whom they were registered. He had made all the necessary transport and accommodation arrangements for them.

As the coach left Jeddah carrying the pilgrims, they recited in Arabic words used by pilgrims for centuries, known as the **Talbiya**:

> Labbaika allahumma labbaik, labbaika la sharika laka labbaik,
> innal hamda wanni'mata laka wal mulk, la sharika lak.

> 'I am present Lord, I am present, I am present, you who has no partner, I am present, all the blessings are for you; the universe is yours. You have no partner.'

Mr and Mrs Ahmad had also recited these words after changing their clothes at Gatwick; now they seemed to take on an even greater meaning for them as, in company with so many other pilgrims, they drew near to Mecca.

Already there was a feeling of excitement among the pilgrims which increased as they covered the 45 minutes from Jeddah to Mecca. As they approached the outskirts of the city, they murmured a prayer together: 'Lord grant that we may dwell here and may the means of our stay be free from all suspicion.'

When we asked Mr Ahmad what the meaning of this prayer was, he told us that Muslims would regard their Hajj as of no spiritual benefit if they had paid for it by dishonest means or had deprived their families in order to make the journey. This is one of the reasons why they were careful not to leave behind any unpaid bills or debts.

As soon as the pilgrims arrived in Mecca, they made their way to the Sacred Mosque to perform what is called **tawaf**; this consists of circling the Kaaba seven times. Before entering the Mosque, however, **wudu** has to be carried out. This is the ritual washing which is always done by Muslims before prayer. Pilgrims entering the Sacred Mosque for the first time on Hajj enter through the gate known as **Bab Al Salam**, i.e. 'the gate of peace' or 'gate of salvation'. As the Ahmads and their fellow pilgrims passed through this entrance, there, ahead of them, they caught their first glimpse of the sacred Kaaba, a simple, cube-shaped building, draped in black cloth. Hundreds of other pilgrims were already moving around it, and the feeling of excitement reached a new pitch. As they passed through into the large, open courtyard, the pilgrims recited together:

> O Lord, grant this house greater honour, respect and awe; and grant those who respect it and make pilgrimage to it, peace and forgiveness. O Lord! Thou art the peace. Peace is from thee. So greet us on the Day of Judgement with the greeting of peace.

The group of pilgrims linked arms so that they would be able to keep together in the crowd moving around the Kaaba, and in this way they began their first circling of the building. This is always done by keeping the Kaaba on the left, which means circling it in an anti-clockwise direction. The circle begins at the corner in which the Black Stone is set. Pilgrims are eager to touch it or kiss it; many say it represents the right hand of Allah to whom they are giving their loyalty. Those who cannot get close enough to touch the stone may even throw a kiss in its direction and raise their right hand, reciting, 'In the name of God; God is most great.'

We asked Mr Ahmad if this touching or kissing the stone was not a kind of idolatry. 'Surely,' we asked, 'you are not addressing your prayers to a stone?' 'Certainly not!' he replied, 'Indeed, the second leader of Islam, after Muhammad, the Caliph Umar, said, "I know you are nothing but a stone and that you have no power to do either good or evil; if I had not seen the prophet greet you like this, I would not do so." '

Once the pilgrims had circled the Kaaba seven times, they emerged from the crowd at the Black Stone corner and made their way

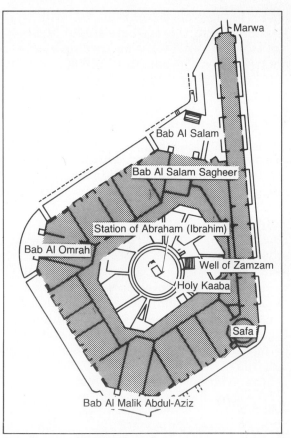

Plan of the Great Mosque

The Kaaba

across to the Well of Zamzam. You will remember that this is where Hagar and her son Ishmael found water, according to the ancient story. The pilgrims were given some of this rich mineral water to quench their thirst after their exhausting encircling of the Kaaba. Their thoughts turned to how God had saved these their ancestors and how Muhammad also had quenched his thirst at this same well. They prayed inwardly as they drank, that God would provide for their needs just as he had for Hagar and Ishmael.

Safa and Marwa

From the Zamzam well, pilgrims then walk, or jog if they are able, between the hills of Safa and Marwa. You will remember that these are the hills between which Hagar ran seven times, searching for water to quench her thirst after she was left by Abraham. Pilgrims remember this part of the story by going between the hills seven times as Hagar did; this part of the Hajj is called the **sa'y**.

Mr and Mrs Ahmad told us that nowadays, for the convenience of the pilgrims and for their safety since the numbers are so great, a covered walkway has been constructed between the hills and it is now, in fact, part of the whole mosque complex. One-way passages have been made so that the pilgrims go by one to Safa and return by the other to Marwa. Between these are two other passageways for wheelchairs to carry those who are unable to cover the distance on foot. It is approximately 460 yards from Safa to Marwa, so covering this distance seven times means a distance of about one and a half miles. Mr Ahmad said that he and his wife, along with all the hundreds of other pilgrims, recited prayers as they jogged between the two points and he felt especially close to God in this sacred place.

Task 6
Write down what you understand by:
  (a) tawaf
  (b) Bab al Salam
  (c) mutawwif

(d) sa'y
(e) wudu.

Task 7
It has often been said in our multi-faith society that meeting with people of other faiths enriches our lives, giving us greater understanding of other people's religion and of our own. Imagine a discussion between someone who takes that view, with one who supports the view that Muslims are right not to allow non-Muslims into Mecca.

The Plain of Arafat

The next important stage of the Hajj is on the Plain of Arafat which is approximately 12 miles east of Mecca. Whereas the circling of the Kaaba can be done by pilgrims at any time during the pilgrimage season, this part of the Hajj only takes place on the ninth day of the pilgrimage month, Dhu-el-Hijja, and if a pilgrim does not share in this, then he cannot regard himself as having completed the Hajj.

The Ahmads, like many other pilgrims, spent the evening and night of the eighth day at Mina which is about four miles from Mecca. After the dawn prayers, they boarded their coach which was to take them the remaining eight miles to Arafat. The coach edged out into a solid mass of traffic of all kinds of vehicles – cars, lorries, buses, many with pilgrims sitting on the roof, some shading themselves from the hot morning sun with umbrellas. The traffic moved slowly, and everyone was eager to reach their destination where they would pray and meditate until sunset.

In the middle of this vast plain of Arafat is a hill known as 'The Mount of Mercy; here, in the year 632 CE, the Prophet Muhammad preached his last sermon to his followers, while making the pilgrimage with them. The Plain of Arafat is about two and a half square miles, and on this day the whole area is crowded with tents and people. The pilgrim is reminded that he is one of about two million Muslims who have come to stand in this sacred place and offer their devotion to God.

We asked Mr and Mrs Ahmad about their visit to Arafat.

Our question: Did you get anywhere near the Mount of Mercy when you went to Arafat?

Answer: No! We could see it, of course, but we were some distance from it. We were not far from the Mosque of Namira which is by the entrance to Arafat. At this mosque we heard a sermon given by the leader of the pilgrimage; such a sermon is always given each year to commemorate the sermon given by the Prophet Muhammad on his last visit to Arafat. We also celebrated the midday prayers here at this mosque.

Our question: Can you remember much of the sermon which you heard on your visit?

Answer: Oh Yes! In fact it reinforced for us the message Muhammad gave in his last sermon. We were reminded of our duty to care about other people and to treat them as we would like to be treated ourselves. We were told to be on our guard against the 'Evil One' and to remember that one day we would have to answer to God for all our deeds on earth. The brotherhood of Muslims was also stressed and, because we were in company that day with about two million fellow Muslims, we felt that the words about brotherhood were especially important.

Our question: If it is not too personal a question, may we ask what you were thinking about during what must have seemed a very long stay at Arafat?

Answer: I am happy to answer your question, but first let me say that it did not seem a long stay! It was such a moving experience to be there that it seemed as if the time passed all too quickly. After all, the Prophet is reported to have said, 'the Hajj is Arafat', so being there is even more important than circling the Holy Kaaba or kissing the Black Stone.

Crowds at Arafat

What did I think about? Mainly I was expressing regret for the wrongs in my life and seeking Allah's forgiveness. There are many prayers which we Muslims can use at this time, many of them coming from Muhammad himself. Here is one which I used:

> 'O Allah, I have done great wrong to myself. There is none to forgive the sins but thou only. Grant me pardon from thyself, have mercy upon me for thou art much forgiving and compassionate.'

Silently praying such prayers and reading some passages from the Qur'an made the time at Arafat an experience I shall never forget. Somehow, I felt as never before that Allah was near me and that he would truly forgive me.

Our question: Have you any other outstanding memory of Arafat?

Answer: Yes I have! I can still see the faces of some of my fellow pilgrims who stood near me. Some of them had tears streaming down their cheeks and I knew by the expressions on many faces that being here, while being a duty for every Muslim, was much, much more: it was a sacred privilege and a great honour, and I knew I was not alone in being deeply moved by being present.

Task 8

There is an old Muslim legend which tells of a man who saved for a long time so that he could make the Hajj. At last he was able to set out on the journey with a few friends. One day he came across an old woman who was very poor indeed and he felt so sorry for her that he gave her food and money. By doing this, however, he could no longer afford to continue his journey to Mecca. He made the excuse to his friends that he was unwell and said he would follow later; in fact, he returned home sadly. When his friends returned from Hajj, they congratulated him on making the pilgrimage! He explained that he had not been able to go, but his friends only smiled and said they had seen him many times and, in a vision, Allah had told them he had made a wonderful pilgrimage and Allah was well pleased with him!

(a) Imagine the struggle in the man's mind before he decided to give help to the woman. Write down what you think his thoughts may have been. How do you think he felt afterwards as he returned home? How do you think he felt when his friends returned and congratulated him?

(b) What does this old story suggest to you about the importance of the Hajj?

Mina and the Day of Eid-ul-Adha

At sunset the pilgrims boarded their coach and were taken back along the road leading to Mecca, but only as far as the hill of Muzalifah which is approximately four miles from Arafat. Here they said prayers and most of them, after prayers, gathered 49 pebbles which they would use over the next few days when they returned to Mina.

The next day, the tenth day of the month Dhu-el-Hijja, is known as the Day of Sacrifice and is celebrated by Muslims all over the world as the festival of sacrifice, **Eid-ul-Adha**. The main event to which their minds turn on this day is when Abraham attempted to sacrifice his son, Ishmael, to God, but was shown that he should sacrifice a ram instead. Muslims everywhere also think of their fellow Muslims who are making the Hajj and observe special ceremonies within their own communities.

Pilgrims celebrate this festival at Mina, so the Ahmads and their companions travelled the short distance there where they spent three nights and carried out certain rites.

In Mina there are three sacred stone pillars known as Jamarat-al-Aqabah (the great pillar), Jamarat-al-Wusta (the middle pillar) and Jamarat-al-Sugra (the small pillar). There is a popular legend that these pillars mark the path followed by Abraham and Ishmael when they were travelling to the place where Abraham attempted to sacrifice his son. The legend says that Satan appeared to Abraham three times, trying to persuade him to disobey God's command; these pillars are said to mark the places where Abraham was so tempted.

Part of the ritual followed by pilgrims during their stay at Mina is that they throw the pebbles gathered previously at these pillars. Mr Ahmad told us that to make this possible for the large numbers of pilgrims, there are two levels, an upper and a lower, from which the stones can be thrown. He said that on the first day at Mina, seven pebbles are thrown at the great pillar and on each of the next two days seven are thrown at each of the three pillars. This seemed to us a strange ritual, especially when compared with the very spiritual activities of the previous day at Arafat, so we asked for an explanation.

We were told, 'It is not really out of keeping with what we did at Arafat. There we were praying for forgiveness and becoming more aware of the wrongs in our lives. When we stone the pillars we are symbolising our hatred of evil and expressing our desire to make a complete break from all that is wrong. These pillars remind us of Abraham being tempted by Satan – it is said that Abraham and Ishmael answered the temptations by throwing stones at Satan, so we do the same.

'The stones are supposed to be small pebbles but many pilgrims feel so strongly about resisting evil that they show this by throwing bigger stones. I also saw many sandals and other objects being hurled at the pillars as pilgrims tried to express their hatred of evil.'

Mrs Ahmad said, 'It was also interesting to see the expressions on many faces as this rite was carried out. Clearly this was no meaningless ritual for most pilgrims, but a very real display of their hatred of evil and their desire to live better lives'.

The other important ritual to be performed on the Eid day is the sacrifice of an animal, usually a sheep or a goat. This is to commemorate Abraham's sacrifice of a ram when he realised that God did not want the sacrifice of his son. Bedouin tribesmen lead large herds of animals into the area to be sold to the pilgrims; and often a number of pilgrims share the cost of one animal, if they feel they cannot afford one by themselves. The animals are slaughtered either by the pilgrims or by butchers employed by them. Part of the meat is cooked and eaten at Mina, but the Qur'an lays down that a large portion of it must be given to the poor. Clearly, with the large number of pilgrims who now make the Hajj, the amount sacrificed is considerably more than the local needy

Stoning the Pillars

people can use, so a refrigerated store has been built at Mina so that meat which cannot be distributed to the poor immediately can be given later.

Mrs Ahmad said, 'By offering a sacrifice, we are giving thanks to God, but we are also showing that we are ready to give up some of our worldly possessions and are willing to share with those less fortunate than ourselves.'

We asked if all that occupied the three days at Mina was stoning the pillars and offering a sacrifice. Mrs Ahmad replied, 'No! Let me summarise the activities for you.

1 Arrival at Mina early on the tenth day of Dhu-el-Hijja.
2 Visit the Great Pillar and throw seven pebbles.
3 Sacrifice an animal.
4 Men have the head shaved (some only have their hair trimmed, but head shaving is preferred). Pilgrims also bathe and put on their normal clothes instead of the pilgrimage dress. This is to symbolise a return to 'ordinary life' after the restrictions of the Hajj.
5 Return to Mecca for a brief visit to circle the Kaaba again as we had done in the first stages of the Hajj.
6 Return to Mina
7 On each of the remaining two days, visit the three pillars and throw seven pebbles at each.

'During these days, of course, we also observed the usual times of prayer. Personally, I also spent a great deal of time just reflecting on the experiences of the Hajj and realising how deeply my faith had been strengthened by making this journey.'

Farewell to Mecca

The final act of every pilgrim is a return to the Sacred Mosque at Mecca to perform another **tawaf**, i.e. a circling of the Kaaba. This is known by many as 'tawaf al-wada', the farewell tawaf. Some Muslims however, prefer to call it 'tawaf as-sadr', the departure

tawaf. We asked Mr Ahmad what this different name really meant. He replied, 'What it means is that if we talk of the farewell tawaf, it suggests an ending; if we talk of the departure tawaf, it suggests that it is more like a beginning, a setting out. Of course, the tawaf does mark the end of this great experience of Hajj, but we should also see it as a beginning – we are setting out from the Hajj to live better lives because our faith has been strengthened by being on Hajj, and we have a deeper commitment to follow the teaching of the Qur'an and to serve God.'

Our question: Was this final tawaf an important experience for you?

Answer: Oh yes! I found it just as moving as on my first visit at the beginning of Hajj. Indeed, perhaps it was even more meaningful, for having performed all the other rites of Hajj, I felt more deeply involved in my faith than ever before.

Our question: Were you, at any time, close enought to the Kaaba to be able to touch the Black Stone?

Answer: No! Every time I was performing tawaf, the crowds were so great that I was always some distance away. I talked to a few pilgrims who performed tawaf many times at the end of Hajj, hoping every time that they would be close enough to touch the stone. Personally I did not feel it was so important. I do not think my feeling of closeness to God could have been any greater than it was.

Our question: Will you ever make the Hajj again?

Answer: I really don't know! Of course, I would like to go again. I am told by Muslims who have made several visits that on every visit they feel even closer to Allah and learn more about their faith and way of life. Others say that to go once or even twice in a lifetime makes it more special. The most important time, of course, is the first because it is then that you fulfil your duty and obey Allah's command to make the pilgrimage.

Our question: Would you say that making the Hajj was in any way difficult?

Answer: Yes, in many ways it was; there were many rules to obey. For example, I normally smoke, but this is forbidden on Hajj. I must say, however, that even my desire to smoke was forgotten when I was caught up in the exciting atmosphere of the Hajj. Also the heat was hard to bear, especially coming from our climate in Britain. The heat and the walking around so much left me feeling quite exhausted at times. Difficult? Yes, but it was all worth it!

Our question: Finally, as you look back on the Hajj, what would you say was your most outstanding memory?

Answer: That is a complicated question for there are so many memories. Certainly seeing the Kaaba is something I will never forget and I will see it in my mind every time I face towards it to pray. I think perhaps the most vivid memory is of the faces of fellow pilgrims at Arafat, so clearly moved by the experience, and the sound heard again and again throughout the Hajj of pilgrims chanting the Talbiya: 'I am present Lord, I am present, I am present, you who has no partner, I am present, all the blessings are for you; the universe is yours. You have no partner.'

Task 9

The following relate to stages of the pilgrimage in which every pilgrim is involved:

Ihram   Kaaba   Zamzam
Safa and Marwa   Mina   Arafat
Muzdalifah   Mina   Mecca

Make up a table of two columns with each of the stages on the left-hand side and 'what the pilgrim must do' next to it.

Task 10

(a) Produce a short brochure about the Hajj for a travel agent to give to prospective travellers.

(b) Design an advertising poster for a travel agent who specialises in making arrangements for pilgrims going on Hajj.

Medina

Although it not a compulsory part of the Hajj, most pilgrims go to Medina from Mecca before returning home. You will remember that this is the city where Muhammad met with great success after he left Mecca. It was in Medina that the first Islamic state was set up and where rules were established for life in such a community. Indeed, the move to Medina is regarded as such an important event that the Islamic calendar starts from the day it took place. It was in Medina also that Muhammad was buried when he died in the year 632 CE. The Prophet said that Hajjis should visit him after the pilgrimage, and they believe that by going there they are bearing witness to the fact that he was God's messenger.

In company with many other pilgrims, the Ahmads travelled to Medina some 200 miles north of Mecca. They found it an attractive city and, although it was very busy, felt more relaxed than they had in Mecca; there was not the same urgency to visit the holy places as there had been in the more important centre of Mecca. They stressed to us that being at Medina is not in any sense part of Hajj. 'Going there,' they said, 'is like going as the guest of the Prophet; he asked us to visit him and that is what we do.'

Our question: We have talked before about Muslims being forbidden to do anything which might seem like idolatry, and you convinced us that kissing the Black Stone is not an act of idolatry. Is there not a serious danger that by visiting this place so closely associated with Muhammad, and especially going to his tomb, you are treating him rather like an idol?

Answer: No! We are showing our deep love and respect for him and our commitment to the faith and way of life which we learned from him, but certainly we are not treating him like a god! In Mecca, we did not even visit places connected with events in his life, such as his birthplace or the house where he lived.

Exterior of Prophet's Mosque, Medina

In Medina, however, we did visit famous sites, places where important followers of the Prophet are buried and, of course, the tomb of Muhammad himself.

At all these places there are notices warning us that we must not kneel or bow down at them, and a few policemen are present to make sure that this rule is obeyed. However famous and important people are within our faith, they are to be respected not worshipped.

Our question: Tell us about your visit to the Prophet's Tomb, for that must have been the highlight of your stay in Medina.

Answer: Yes, it certainly was! The Prophet's Mosque is a magnificent building with beautiful mosaics and stone carvings. As we admired its beauty, we were also mindful of the fact that originally on this site stood a very simple place where Muhammad lived and preached and prayed. As we entered, we recited, 'In the name of God, the Merciful, the Compassionate; from God alone comes all strength and power. God bless our Lord Muhammad, thy Servant and thy Prophet.'

In the centre of the mosque is the minbar; a **minbar** is a series of a few steps and is used as a pulpit in a mosque. It is believed that the Prophet used to pray in this exact spot where the minbar now stands. We felt honoured to be able to pray in such a place.

As we entered that part of the mosque containing the Prophet's Tomb, we said a simple greeting, 'Peace be upon you O Prophet, and the mercy and blessings of God.' It is like greeting a well loved friend.

No one bowed and we were careful not to walk around the grave as we did around the Kaaba. We are not worshipping Muhammad, but only Allah. Here we are praying God to bless Muhammad and reward him for all that he has done. Our friends, back home, knowing we would come to this place, had asked us to give their greetings to the Prophet; this we did quietly as we stood by the tomb.

Our question: How did you feel as you stood there by the tomb?

Answer: We felt very moved and tears came to our eyes. They were not tears of sadness, but tears of joy forced out by a feeling of closeness to the great Prophet, and because of him and his message, closeness to God.

We also found ourselves remembering what we had been told about the day when Muhammad died. Abu Bakr, his great friend and close helper entered the place where the body of the Prophet was lying covered with a striped cloth. He uncovered the Prophet's face and gently murmured, 'Your career, O Muhammad, is well accomplished.' Abu Bakr then faced the crowd outside, and said to them, 'O people, whoever worshipped Muhammad, know that Muhammad is dead. But whoever worshipped Allah, know that Allah is alive, for Allah cannot die.'

82

Our question: We understand it is traditional for pilgrims to bring home some gifts for family and friends.

Answer: Yes, and Medina is the place where these are usually bought. We both enjoyed looking through the many shops in the bazaars of the city. We knew that whatever gifts we brought, they would bring pleasure to our family, coming from such a holy place. We wanted some of our gifts to be useful, so we brought such items as a bag for our daughter; we also wanted others, however, to be items to do with our faith, so we brought some prayer mats and prayer beads.

Our question: We are most grateful to you for sharing your experience of the Hajj with us. You have certainly convinced us that it was an experience of a lifetime! Is there any final word that you would say to us about such a journey?

Answer: Yes, when we look back on our pilgrimage, we are aware of the importance of our past, and such contact with the past can strengthen our faith for today and encourages us to go on trusting Allah for the future.

Task 1

The visit to Medina is very different to the visit to Mecca. Explain the ways in which it is particularly different.

Task 2

(a) Why do you think a devout Muslim would especially appreciate a gift brought back from pilgrimage?

(b) Which gifts would be most appreciated from a religious point of view? Give reasons for your answer.

Task 3

Why are Muslims always careful to avoid anything might seem like idolatry? Outline ways in which they especially show this avoidance of idolatry when making the pilgrimage.

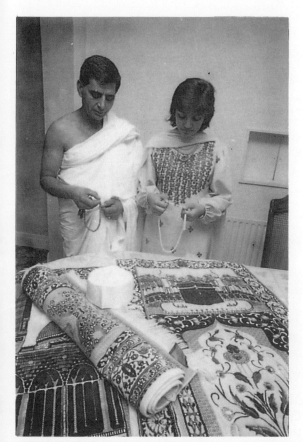

Gifts brought home by pilgrims

5   Sikh Pilgrimages

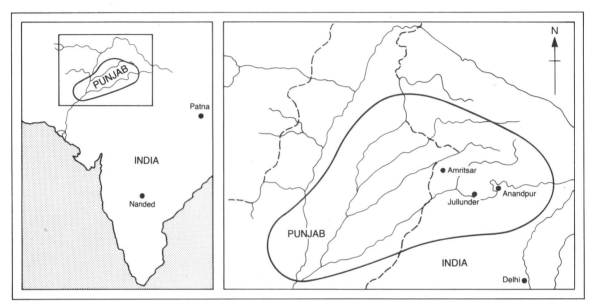

Map of Punjab

Amritsar

Amritsar is an important city in the Punjab, an Indian state which lies to the north-west of the country. This city attracts Sikhs from all over the world, for to them it is a particularly holy place. It is made holy by the presence of a beautiful building, popularly known as the Golden Temple because both the dome and the upper part of the building are covered in gold plated copper sheets.

When the temple was built in the seventeenth century it was called the **Harimandir**, 'the Temple of God'; today, Sikhs call it the **Darbar Sahib**, 'the Lord's Court'.

Pilgrimage for Sikhs is not a religious duty in the same way as making the Hajj is for

View of the golden Temple

Muslims, but devoted members of the Sikh faith do have the strong ambition to visit the temple and bathe in the holy water which surrounds it, at least once in their lifetime.

The Pilgrimage Story

The Sikh religion was founded by Guru Nanak in the fifteenth century. At that time, the main religions in the Punjab where he lived were Hinduism and Islam. Nanak saw some good in both these faiths but was also critical of some of their teachings. He taught that God is 'One' and that he can be found by all who seek him, for all men and women are equal. His new teaching appealed to people from all walks of life and many Hindus and Muslims became his followers. Before his death, Nanak chose one of his followers to lead the Sikhs and be 'Guru' after him, and this tradition continued until by 1708 there had been ten gurus in all. As Sikhism grew and developed, these gurus had to make sure that Sikhs were strong and united, and that they followed a particular way of life, obeying the teaching of Guru Nanak. One way to do this was to build centres where Sikhs could live, work and worship together.

It was Ram Das, the fourth guru, who discovered the perfect place for such a community. On one of his journeys, he came across a low-lying site with a pool and shady trees. The beauty of the place attracted him; so did the fact that many caravans travelling to the north-west frontier passed through it. He felt this was an ideal place which would attract people to live and work, with plenty of opportunity for trade and business, as well as the chance to live as a community following their common faith.

Ram Das called on Sikhs to help build their new town which at first was known as Ramdaspur. Once the community was set up and the town began to prosper, the guru decided that the Sikhs should have their own holy place in which to bathe. Guru Nanak had always risen early and bathed before worship; the Sikhs had followed his example but had usually, like the Hindus, bathed in one or other of India's holy rivers. Since there was a pool in Ramdaspur it was a simple matter to enlarge it for the holy purpose the Sikhs had in mind.

Digging began on 6 November 1573, and

Guru Nanak

Guru Ram Das

the work continued until, in place of the small pool, they had a large tank. On its completion, the guru held a celebration at which he said, 'He who calls himself a Sikh should rise early, take a bath and make an effort to wash in this pool of nectar.'

Ram Das was succeeded as guru by his son, Arjan; he was a great spiritual leader who made sure that Ramdaspur would be a holy place for ever. The tank built by his father was made more permanent, and while this was being done, Arjan designed a temple which was to be built in the centre of the tank. The foundation stone was laid in 1589 and by 1601 the temple was complete. The Sikhs were amazed at its beauty – such a splendid temple in the middle of a huge tank standing as a symbol of the Sikh faith was

The tank at Amritsar

indeed something to be admired, and it drew visitors from all over India. Guru Arjan thanked God for this achievement saying, 'He who bathes in this tank of the saints receives supreme bliss. He dies not, nor comes, nor goes, for he dwells only upon the Lord's name.' The town was now renamed **Amritsar**, 'the pool of immortality'.

Arjan decided to look for other places in which to set up Sikh communities. While he was absent from Amritsar some others tried to seize power; they unsettled the minds of the Sikhs of Amritsar by changing the words handed down by the first four gurus. Arjan returned to assert his leadership and establish the true Sikh faith begun by Guru Nanak. He decided to put together the hymns of the gurus so that Sikhs would have one book which contained their original teaching; these hymns would tell of one God and the unity and equality of all people.

To this collection of the writings of the earlier gurus, Arjan added his own words and those of some Hindu and Muslim saints. To emphasise its importance, the Adi Granth, as the book came to be called, was placed in the temple at Amritsar in 1604, where Arjan bowed low before it to show that it contained the true word of God.

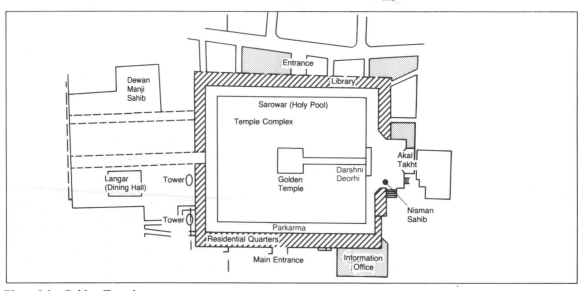

Plan of the Golden Temple

Years later, the tenth guru, Gobind Singh, added some of his father's words to the holy book. he also decreed that Sikhs would not have another guru after him: from now on, the holy book would be their leader and teacher. It then became known as the **Guru Granth Sahib** and wherever Sikhs worship, whether at Amritsar or anywhere else in the world, they honour the book and live by its teachings.

town. Many, however, were unwilling to come and live in Amritsar because of its position. It was Guru Arjan, the sixth guru, who enlarged the tank, begun by Ram Das, and lined it with gold. He also designed the Temple to be built in the centre of the tank. The foundation stone was laid in 1601. He also placed the holy book, which was called the Guru Granth Sahib in the temple in 1604.

Task 1

The following paragraph contains ten deliberate mistakes. Rewrite it putting in the correct information.

> Amritsar is situated in southern India. The city is famous for its Golden Temple, the Darbar Sahib which means 'the Temple of God'. Pilgrimage is a religious duty which all Sikhs are expected to obey, so visitors flock to Amritsar from all over the world. It was Ram Das, the fifth guru, who decided that the site on which Amritsar now stands would be an ideal place for a Sikh

Task 2

(a) Guru Ram Das and Guru Arjan believed it was important to have a special centre for the Sikh faith. Explain their reasons for this.

(b) What do you think are the advantages and disadvantages, for any faith, of having such a centre?

Task 3

Water has always been symbolic in most religions. Explain why it is such a common symbol and particularly explain why it is seen as important to Sikhs.

Musicians at the Golden Temple

Visiting the Golden Temple

Mr Kulbinder Singh and his family visited the Golden Temple in 1983. In spite of the passing of the years, Mr Singh still vividly remembers their pilgrimage. 'Once you go to this place,' he told us, 'you feel that you never want to leave it!'

When we asked him to tell us about the visit, he replied 'We planned to go to India to visit relatives in Jullunder, but my father particularly wanted to visit some of the Sikh holy shrines on this journey. I also had longed to bathe in the tank at Amritsar so it was decided: we visited our relatives and also went to Amritsar!'

Our question: Is there a problem about accommodation for visitors to Amritsar?

Answer: No! There are many rest houses in the temple complex; any visitor can stay free of charge for three nights. There is a large dining hall, similar to the langar in our place of worship, the gurdwara, at home. Here food is served, also free of charge, but visitors help to prepare and serve the food.

Our question: What was your first impression of the temple?

Answer: We were part of a large crowd heading in the direction of the temple. Even before we reached it, we could hear the **kirtan**, the hymns sung by the temple musicians, for their singing is relayed through a sound system to the whole temple complex. As we approached we found many fellow Sikhs sitting listening by the main entrance.

Before passing through the main gateway, we removed our shoes and washed our feet; my wife and daughter covered their heads. All these actions are to show our respect as this is a holy place. To enter an important building you often have to go up steps – at the Golden Temple, you go down steps! It is said that as you go down you are humbling yourself before God. We paused at the bottom of the steps to gaze in wonder at what lay before us! The temple rose from the waters of the tank like a peaceful island: it glittered and shone in the sunlight casting a golden reflection in the water. It is a sight I shall never forget!

Our question: We believe it is important to bathe in the tank. Will you tell us a little more about this practice?

Answer: When the temple was completed, Guru Arjan said that the Sikhs need not go to any other place of pilgrimage, for in these waters they would find complete contentment. So the first action of any visitor is to bathe as the guru commanded. Once we had taken in the splendid sight of the Golden Temple we all bathed in the waters. Since we stayed for three nights, I took the opportunity to bathe quite frequently. The occasions which are most memorable are those when I rose very early in the morning and joined fellow Sikhs in bathing and in reciting the Sikh morning prayer, the **Japji**. An early morning mist was rising from the water, the air was full of the sound of prayers being chanted and there was a feeling of complete devotion to God; at these times I certainly experienced the peace and contentment which the guru had promised.

Our question: Is the tank very deep?

Answer: Yes, I think it is about five metres at its deepest point. It is also very large – 150 metres square. It is always full because a canal was built to bring a regular flow of water into it. Although it is large and deep, many precautions are taken to ensure that it is safe to bathe.

Our question: Will you tell us now about the Golden Temple itself?

Answer: Going into the temple was, of course, a very important part of our visit. There is only one way to reach the temple and that is by a single bridge; this is another sign of the emphasis Sikhs put on the equality of everyone – rich and poor, humble and great, all must come in the same way! As we passed through the entrance to the bridge we paused to look at the huge gates of the Darshni Deorhi, the gatehouse which protects the entrance. The temple has a walkway all around it.

Bridge at Golden Temple

There are four doors, one on each side of the temple; these all stand open showing that everyone is welcome to enter. As we walked round we glanced in at each entrance before going into the large, ground floor room. The main feature which met our eyes was the holy book, resting under a gorgeous canopy. Our first action was to bow low before the book, which is our guru, and then we put our offerings on a large white sheet spread out in front of the canopy, before taking our place among the congregation already seated on the floor. I lost all sense of time as we sat there listening to the ragis singing the hymns from the Guru Granth Sahib – time no longer seemed to matter! While we sat there, we were given **karah prashad**, the sweet food which is given in every Sikh act of worship in the presence of the holy book.

When we did leave, it was by the southern door and we came to steps which lead down to the waters of the tank; these particular steps are known as **Har Ki Pauri**. This is an especially holy place for it is said that here Guru Arjan had a vision of God in the form of a labourer, when the temple was being built.

A nearby staircase leads to the second floor of the temple where there is a room known as **Shish Mahal**. It is a beautiful room with many mirrors; some say that our gurus used to sit here in meditation. Nowadays, a continuous reading from the Guru Granth Sahib takes place in this room. Such a continous reading is known as **Akand Path**. This practice is not unique to the Golden Temple; we do it in our own gurdwara at

89

special, happy times such as our festivals, but in the Golden Temple it is always going on.

Our question: Is the temple really as beautiful as it appears in photographs?

Answer: Even more so! It is full of marvellous decorations: hymns of the gurus are inscribed in the walls in letters of gold, the marble walls are also decorated with mirror work, gold leaf, designs of animals, birds and flowers in semi-precious stones. There are also fresco paintings reminding us of the important teaching of our faith, that we can control our human desires by discipline and recitation of the name of God. Words can never convey fully how wonderful this place is!

Shrines around the Temple
Mr Singh went on to tell us how pilgrims walk round the marble walkway after being inside the temple. Here around the tank are a number of places which mark important events in the history of the Sikh faith. There is also a special bathing place for those who are sick; at another point is a tree regarded as sacred, for it was a favourite of the first head priest of the temple and it is now 450 years old! A shrine which particularly impressed the Singh children was the one dedicated to Baba Deep Singh. They had seen pictures of this famous Sikh warrior in their

Interior of Golden Temple

own gurdwara at home, but to be at the spot where he died in the eighteenth century was a great honour. At the time Amritsar was being attacked by enemies of the Sikhs and the temple was being threatened. Deep Singh was then living away from Amritsar and was in fact engaged on writing out a copy of the **Guru Granth Sahib**. When he heard the news about Amritsar, he vowed to defend the temple with his own blood. Other Sikhs rallied round him and fought the invaders. Deep Singh was seriously wounded before he even reached the temple, but battled on. Eventually he died at this spot which is marked by a shrine in his honour.

Task 4
Copy the plan of the Golden Temple on page 86 into your book. Name each place which has been mentioned so far. Write a sentence about each place you have named.

Task 5
The Golden Temple reflects important Sikh beliefs in its design and decoration. Either by drawing a plan, or by describing it in words, design a temple as a centre of pilgrimage for a group of people who hold the following beliefs.
  (a) Mountains are holy.
  (b) God created the world.
  (c) Seven is a sacred number.
  (d) Peace is important.
  (e) Everyone is welcome to worship.
  (f) Animals should be protected as part of God's creation.
  (g) God loves everyone.

Task 6
Think carefully about the Golden Temple complex. Explain what the design tells us about Sikh beliefs.

Special Ceremonies at Amritsar
Mr and Mrs Singh also spoke of some of the special ceremonies they took part in during their pilgrimage. 'We both rose early one morning; we wanted not only to bathe in the

The ceremony at Akal Tàkht

tank but also take part in the ceremony in which the Guru Granth Sahib is taken from the Akal Takht, a building near the gatehouse, where it rests at night. I will tell you more about Akal Takht later when I give you some information about a few other places in India which are important to Sikhs.
  'At 5 a.m. the procession started; hundreds of other pilgrims had gathered and were chanting hynms from the holy book. The Granthi carried the book on his head from the rest-room to the **palki**. The palki is a kind of stretcher on which the holy book is carried in procession: it is gold plated and has velvet cushions on which the book is carefully laid. Flowers were scattered over the Guru Granth Sahib and many pilgrims touched the palki, believing that they would receive the Guru's blessing. The procession was led

The Akal Takht at Amritsar

by a lamp bearer, a standard bearer and a group of musicians. Next came the Guru Granth Sahib itself, resting in the palki and carried high on the shoulders of the bearers; the Granthi followed, waving a chauri over the book. We followed behind, making our way slowly over the bridge, walking on fresh, white sheets which had been laid in honour of the holy book. At the door of the temple the palki was laid down; the Granthi, with great ceremony, placed the book on his head and carried it to the **manji sahib**, the place under the canopy where it rests and from which it is read. The book was opened at random and the Granthi read the hymn on that page to us all. In this way, we Sikhs were listening to the word of God and taking advice about our faith.

'This was a most moving ceremony for us in the calm atmosphere of the early hours of that morning. Every time we see the holy book carried in our own home gurdwara, our minds go back to the scene at Amritsar. We also attended an evening ceremony, known as a **chauki**. After the completion of **Rahiras**, the evening prayer, many of us gathered at the Akal Takht, the building where the Guru Granth Sahib rests at night. From here the evening procession starts, led by a standard bearer, one person who carries a sword and two people carrying torches. We followed the first torch bearer, reciting hymns; others followed the second torch bearer and repeated the hymns sung by our group. In this fashion we walked all the way round the parkarma and eventually, standing outside the temple, we offered **Ardas**, the famous Sikh prayer, part of which is, 'Turn our thoughts, O Khalsa, to the teachings of the Guru Granth Sahib and call on God'. It was a great joy to repeat these words together in such a holy place and we certainly felt that our thoughts were being turned to God and the teachings of our faith.'

Our final question to Mr Singh was to ask him to sum up for us the experience of making such a pilgrimage.

'My faith was certainly strengthened by visiting Amritsar,' Mr Singh said. 'This was partly because of Amritsar itself and all the associations with the roots of our religion; it was also due to the many fine people I met while I was there who shared my faith. Washing in the tank at Amritsar was a memorable experience, but I do not believe that such an act washed away my sins! It was a symbol of my desire to rise above evil myself and avoid temptation in my everyday life. Journeys like this do not of themselves solve problems in one's life, but they are valuable experiences to which one can return in one's own mind. My family and I are certainly very grateful to God that we were able to make this journey and visit this nerve centre of Sikh religion.'

Task 7
Mr Singh said, 'My faith was certainly strengthened by visiting Amritsar.' What

particular aspects of this pilgrimage do you think were most likely to strengthen his faith?

He also mentioned that he met 'many fine people' on pilgrimage. How do you think this would have helped his faith?

The Four Takhts

We remembered that Mr Singh had said he would give us some information about a few other places of importance to Sikhs. He told us, 'There are many quite famous gurdwaras in India which Sikhs visit. Visiting such holy places reminds us of the ideals of our faith, just as the visit to Amritsar does. The most important, however after the Golden Temple, are what are known as the four **Takhts**. These are four centres of authority and if any problems or questions about our religion arise, scholars based in one or other of these Takhts are consulted.'

Our question: Earlier you mentioned the Akal Takht at Amritsar and said you would tell us more about it; is it one of the four?

Answer: Yes, indeed it is. In fact, it is really the most important of the four Takhts and we thought a geat deal about that when we were at Amritsar. You will remember that it is where the Guru Granth Sahib is put to rest each evening. It is a white marble building, five stories high. The fact that it is the resting place for the holy book adds to its importance.

Our question: What does the word Takht mean?

Answer: It means 'throne'. Just as a king or queen gives a decision or a ruling from the throne, so guidance about, for example, a passage from our holy book, is given from the Takht.

This tradition was started in the time of the sixth guru Hargobind. He built a raised platform near the temple and those with problems or questions came to him there. Later a building was put up and meetings of the leaders of the Sikh brotherhood were held there; that practice continues to the present time.

Our question: Is it regarded as a holy place just as the Golden Temple is?

Answer: Yes! We noticed on our visit that outside it were two **nishan sahibs**, i.e. flagpoles with the Sikh flag flying – these mark it out as a gurdwara. Worship takes place here daily just as it does in any other gurdwara.

Most of the decisions made at the Takht are ones affecting the daily life of Sikhs or of the Sikh communities. Such decisions being made in a holy place remind us that religion and everyday life go hand in hand, that politics and religion cannot be separated – a Sikh cannot be a holy man or woman and forget what is happening in the world. Each one must think of God and act for truth and justice.

Now let me tell you briefly about the other three Takhts.

Patna

One is at **Patna**, and this is very special for it marks the birthplace of the tenth guru, Gobind Singh. We honour him for he was guru at a time when Sikhs were losing heart; he led them in their fight for their faith and

Guru Gobind Singh

way of life. He was born on 26 December 1666; a gurdwara was not built in Patna, however, until the eighteenth century. Now it is carefully looked after in memory of the guru who never gave up the fight for truth

Temple at Anandpur

and justice. Besides having a large congregation hall and features which can be found in any gurdwara, this one also has on display various articles which were associated with the guru: among them are his cradle, sandals, sword, and even a copy of the Guru Granth Sahib signed by him. These are very precious to Sikhs as reminders of the guru who was born to serve the faith and who gave his life for it.

Anandpur

Another important Takht is at **Anandpur**. For most of the year it is a quiet, sleepy town, but in the month of March its streets are crowded with visitors. This place is important because here, on 13 April 1699, Guru Gobind Singh formed the **Khalsa**, the brotherhood of Sikhs.'

We had to interrupt Mr Singh to ask why visits were made in March if the Khalsa was formed in April!

He told us that a festival called **Hola Mohalla** occurs in March. The year after he founded the Khalsa, the guru ordered all Sikhs to come to Anandpur and celebrate the Hindu festival of Holi, but to celebrate it in their own distinctive way. To mark the difference from the Hindu festival he gave it the new name of Hola Mohalla. Holi is a fun festival when Hindus indulge in all sorts of pranks; Sikhs, however, were expected to behave in a much more disciplined way. Hola Mohalla means 'place of attack': in 1700 the Khalsa gathered at Anandpur and took part in mock battles and displays of skill as true soldiers of their faith. This tradition is still carried on today. In March each year it is considered an honour if one is able to obey the command of the guru and gather at Anandpur to listen to the reading of the Guru Granth Sahib, sing hymns and re-enact scenes from the days of Guru Gobind Singh. Mr Singh added, 'It is always good to be reminded of the struggles in the past, which have ensured that we, today, are able to carry on our faith and worship God in our way.'

Nanded

The fourth Takht is at **Nanded** and is also associated with the tenth guru, Gobind Singh. He was a great leader who devoted his whole life to the faith and fought many battles to maintain the freedom of his religion. It was therefore a great shock and a matter of deep sadness to Sikhs when he was taken from them.

The story of his death is as follows. In 1708 he was staying at Nanded and, as usual, many flocked to listen to his teaching. Among them was a young man called Jasmaid Khan who pretended to be devoted to the guru's teaching, but was secretly looking for a chance to take Gobind Singh's life.

It was on 20 September 1708 that he found his opportunity. He was present in the congregation around the guru until nightfall. When Gobind Singh retired to his tent to rest, Jasmaid followed him and waited till he was sure the guru would be in bed. He then entered and bowed low before him. Gobind raised his hand in blessing. At once, Jasmaid struck him with a dagger; the guru, as a true Sikh, had his kirpan within reach and struggled to get it. Jasmaid struck again, badly wounding the guru; however, Gobind Singh managed to plunge his kirpan into Jasmaid and kill him. Gobind knew that he would not survive his wounds; he also knew that his death would come as a great shock to the Sikh communities. Who would guide them in the future? He resolved this by placing five coins and a coconut as an offering before the Granth, the holy book, saying 'Have faith in the Holy Granth as your master and consider it the visible manifestation of the gurus. He who has a pure heart will seek guidance from its words.'

Gobind Singh in this way had given the Sikhs a guru who would never change and who would be a constant guide for the future – the Guru Granth Sahib from now on was to be their guru!

Mr Singh told us that the gurdwara at Nanded is especially important since it stands on the place where Gobind Singh died on 7 October 1708. He said, 'This guru is the example for every Sikh and we honour him by reading the Guru Granth Sahib day and night in the gurdwara, just as he told us to do.'

We asked him to sum up for us just how important the Guru Granth Sahib is in the life of a Sikh. He replied, 'When I am in the presence of the Guru Granth Sahib, I stand before my guru. If Jesus came into the room where Christians were gathered, I am sure they would bow before him to honour him; in the same way, I bow before the Guru Granth Sahib, for this is my teacher and it is this that leads me to God. In this holy place of Nanded, on the first floor of the gurdwara, there is always a continuous reading from the Granth in progress. This is to show our high regard for the holy book; it also honours especially the tenth guru who gave it to us.'

Task 1

Copy the map of the northern part of India. Draw an arrow from each of the following to a box at the side of the page in which you summarise briefly why each place is important to Sikhs:
  (a) Amritsar
  (b) Anandpur
  (c) Patna
  (d) Nanded.

Task 2

  (a) Imagine you are a Sikh planning a visit to each of the holy places. Write about your plans under the following headings.
  (i) Places to visit and in what order.
  (ii) Preparations needed (include here practical preparations such as obtaining a visa, but also 'spiritual' preparations for going on such a pilgrimage'.
  (b) You have returned from your pilgrimage and are asked to share the most memorable parts of it with other people. Describe what you think you would say and give reasons why each experience was particularly memorable.

Index